PRAISE FOR *LIVING ON THE SKINNY BRANCHES*

Living on the Skinny Branches is an opportunity to rediscover the joy and passion of your youth by taking courageous action now to transform your life and the world around you.

—Brad Blanton, Ph.D., Author of *Radical Honesty*

"Michael Strasner is one of the most generously insightful people I've ever known. His coaching and mentorship has translated into exponential growth in my life. Michael's depth of human intelligence is an extraordinary gift, and he uses it to empower and inspire people to live to their highest level of excellence. If you are lucky enough to learn from Michael, your life will never be the same. Living on the Skinny Branches is a must-read."

—Quddus Philippe, TV Host (MTV, NBC, ABC, CBS)

"I've seen Michael Strasner in action and I compare his unique style and infectious energy to the motivational guru Tony Robbins. *Living on the Skinny Branches* is a confidence booster for anyone who is committed to producing greater results in their lives. This book will help many people break through their limiting beliefs."

—Maria Marin, Bestselling Author, TV and Radio Personality, named one of the 25 Most Powerful Latinas by *People Magazine* in Spanish

"Michael Strasner is the person who trained, developed, and mentored me to be where I am today. Visionary, caring, passionate, and committed are just a few words to describe Michael. He is the most extraordinary Coach/Trainer and uses his 30 years of experience to see people's potential and pinpoint exactly what stops them from living life to its fullest. Everyone should read Michael's book, *Living on the Skinny Branches*."

—Chris Lee, Transformational Trainer, Partner, and Entrepreneur

"Michael is one of the most powerful leaders in transformation that I've ever met. The bigger our dreams and goals, the more potential adversity comes our way. If you are looking to take your relationships, health, and personal power to the next level. then ' ⋅ 'her than Michael Strasner and the Ski⋅

⋅ntrepreneur and ⋅eatness Podcast

LIVING ON THE SKINNY BRANCHES

FIVE TOOLS TO CREATING POWER, FREEDOM AND A LIFE WORTH LIVING

MICHAEL STRASNER

ISBN-13: 978-0692480885
ISBN-10: 0692480889

For my wife, Hillary, and our kids,
Nicholas, Savannah, Andrew, Haley, and Conner

FREE BONUS MATERIALS

To download your Life on the Skinny Branches personal strategic plan (PSP), newsletter, and more, sign up today at www.michaelstrasner.com/bonus.

ACKNOWLEDGMENTS

THIS BOOK WOULD NOT exist without my wife, love warrior, and muse, Hillary, and our kids, Nicholas, Savannah, Andrew, Haley, and Conner. I love you with all my heart.

To my mom, dad, dad, Larry, Danielle, Candide, Andy, and Missy—thank you. A special thank you goes to Andy for your incredible tech support, and to Larry for your relentless pursuit of all things.

Honorable mentions go to Kevin, Jay, and Danielle for your invaluable contribution to me personally, and for your support as I was writing and editing my book. To Chris, for being my friend and partner in transformation.

Additional thanks to Jim, Buffalo, Cape Cod, B-52's, U2, Wellesley College, the Cobras, Kristi M, Putterham Meadows, Brookline, Red Sox Nation 2004, Father Joe (Senior), George, Eddie, Doug, Beth, Joan Z, Hildi, Jack, Beattie, JPH, Ivette, the Florida Lifespring staff (Sandy, Dania, Lisa K., Julie, Mackey, Bobbi and many others), 200/100/FULL, Impacto Vital Puerto Rico staff (our partner Ivette, Ernesto, Karla, Sarita, Frances and many others), Puerto Rico Vision 1- Vision 106, Impacto Vital Mexico, Ely, all PHD program graduates worldwide, MITT (Margo, Roger, Jimmy, Jaaculyn and many others), Espacio Vital (Perla, Lupita and many others), WE Liderazgo, Nacho, 4-MAR (Alberto, Jesus and many others), M3 (Bernie, Stacy and many others) - the list goes on.

Lisa, thank you for bringing Nicholas and Savannah into the world and giving all of yourself to them.

To the thousands of students I have coached and trained over the last 30 years, it is and has been an honor and privilege to work with you in creating your vision, dreams, and extraordinary results. I believe that I have learned at least as much from you as you have from me, and I will continue my lifelong quest to create the world we all envision.

CONTENTS

INTRODUCTION

YOU MIGHT BE WONDERING what exactly it means to live life on the Skinny Branches. I define it as creating the passion, courage, confidence, and resilience needed to turn your deepest dreams into observable reality—to transform your life by transforming how you see and experience yourself, how you see and experience the world, and ultimately, how the world sees and experiences you. For this to occur, you must learn to harness, redirect, and transform the following: negative energy from past experiences, your fears and insecurities, both real and perceived limitations, tendencies towards survival, the need to be right, and the resistance to abandoning control. The eventual outcome of this process is that you get significantly better at *creating,* at consciously *being a creator who lives in new possibilities* instead of living as an observer or critic of what others have created around you—or, perhaps, in spite of you. You learn to uncover fresh opportunities, to give of yourself in new and empowering ways, to not simply have a vision but to become vulnerable to that vision so that those around you are unexpectedly, and sometimes permanently, inspired. This book is designed to ignite a new spark within you, to move you to go places you have likely never gone before, and to inspire you to fall in love with the unknown. In short, *Living on the Skinny Branches* is about truly creating a life worth living.

Though the metaphor of Skinny Branches will conjure a variety of interpretations depending on what you, the reader, take from it, this book is not only conceptual. The ideas described within can be applied to specific actions within all domains of your life—personal, professional and social. People from all backgrounds and stages of life can benefit from the ideas and techniques that are presented throughout the chapters that follow.

First and foremost, this book is for people who self-identify and are identified by others as *successful* in some recognizable way: people who "make things happen," movers and shakers, innovators, rainmakers, entrepreneurs, as well as anyone who is consciously looking for a deeper purpose in life, committed to producing greater results, and invested in contributing to society in meaningful ways. Maybe you're in search of a more effective way to empower and grow the most important relationships in your life. Maybe you'd like to become the kind of leader who not only inspires other people but also develops and creates leadership within them. Or maybe you're searching for the best way to reignite your own fire and drive, and to experience renewed clarity and confidence towards your most challenging personal goals.

This book is for professionals who are hungry to learn and looking to gain an edge. Maybe you've received an excellent education, earned the appropriate degrees, made enough money to live comfortably, and achieved all the tangible things that our society says should bring you success and happiness, but something is still missing—something you can't quite put your finger on—and you're not sure why. If you're being honest with yourself, you're thinking, "*If this is all that life is supposed to be, this isn't it.*" You are certain there must be something more meaningful left to experience and something more significant left to achieve in your life.

Young people and college students will benefit greatly from reading this book, as you are passionately committed to pursuing and living your dreams without boundaries and limitations, whether they are self-imposed or not. It's for anyone who is not satisfied with the status quo, with the restrictions placed by their parents, or with following the path laid out for them by other

well-meaning people and institutions. Maybe you want to experience the precious nature of being young, alive, and of truly being
your own person. Becoming someone who makes decisions that
are genuine expressions of who you are and what you want. You
want to turn your life into an example of what's possible for others and make your life extraordinary by interrupting the human
tendency to be lazy and unmotivated, the tendency to settle
for mediocrity.

You could also be someone who is struggling in any specific
area of life: with your business or career, with your relationships,
with personal health, with financial abundance, with spiritual
awareness, or with community activism. Maybe you haven't yet
been able to resolve a persistent or reoccurring breakdown—an
issue or failure—no matter what you do. Maybe you would like to
connect or reconnect with an estranged family member but don't
know how or where to begin. Or maybe you realize that you have
blind spots in your vision of life, and you're interested in seeing the world from fresh perspectives by putting on a new set of
lenses.

This book is for that grandmother who has had a lifelong dream
of being a writer but has never pursued it. Maybe you didn't think
that you were good enough. Maybe you didn't think anyone
would care about what you had to say. Or maybe you've spent
your entire life taking care of other people and always believed
that making time for yourself was never as important as making
time for others—until now.

Whoever you are—whether you're young or old, an entrepreneur with an established business or someone who is just starting
out—if you have a vision and purpose in life and are committed to
seeing it through, then this book can be the springboard that sup-
ports and guides you to places you've never actually gone before.
It can provide you with the inspiration, the clarity, and the courage to go out and live on the Skinny Branches of your life in ways
that you've never before imagined. It will teach you the steps to

take as you venture out, as well as teach you how to self-correct and get up when you fall, how to learn from your experiences and keep moving forward with an ever-increasing sense of purpose. The Skinny Branches of the tree are different for everyone. They don't necessarily require you do something that evokes a heightened sense of fear, such as jumping out of an airplane or walking on a bed of hot coals. Nor do they necessarily require you to reach for an unprecedented accomplishment, such as building a multi-million-dollar company from nothing. While these are examples of Skinny Branch endeavors, you can experience significant levels of passion, courage, and confidence just by doing simple things in your everyday life, like expressing yourself honestly in your relationships, volunteering your time at a non-profit organization or at your child's school, even by simply taking a moment to connect with and acknowledge the barista who serves you coffee every morning. The significance of Skinny Branch living is all a matter of perspective.

As an example, my brother Larry leads a very rich life. He is not rich because of his income or net worth. Instead, he is rich in ways that cannot be quantified. His actual worth is primarily a function of *who* he is and not *what* he has. The quality of his relationships with his wife and children, with his siblings and his friends, and with people in general, is extraordinary. Larry always makes time to be fully present, in heart, mind, body, and spirit, for whomever he is with at any given moment. He would literally give the shirt off his back for even a stranger. He exudes kindness and compassion and his genuine expression of interest towards others makes him an exceptional role model for his five children and all their friends. Anyone who knows him will tell you that as a father, Larry is deeply connected and engaged with each of his children. His version of being on the Skinny Branches is that he is consistent in these behaviors even when others around him are not, or when others might view his behaviors as weird or unnecessary. Larry creates a life worth living through the unconditional way he treats all people, regardless of differences.

It's his state of *being*, not his possessions, that make him wealthy beyond measure, and this is the life that Larry always dreamed he would create for himself. It is exactly what he wants to be—true to himself, regardless of what others may say.

My sister Danielle also leads a rich life. Like most teachers, she is vastly underpaid and sometimes under appreciated, but that does not prevent her from creating a genuinely rich life. Danielle is simply amazing at what she does. She loves every single one of her students. She is making a significant and permanent difference in their lives, which could never be sufficiently appreciated by her or anyone else. For her, living on the Skinny Branches is about producing extraordinary results *through others* in a very conscientious way—results that will likely not be fully realized for many years to come. For some, Danielle's job as a teacher may seem like nothing special. For her, it's exactly where she wants to be and *who* she wants to be, and that is reflected in the *way* she goes about her job. It's reflected in the way she relates to her students and their parents, to her fellow educators, and to everyone within her community. She is not an average, ordinary teacher. She is a humble and quiet leader, which makes her a unique demonstration of what it means to create a life worth living.

So what does creating a life worth living mean to you? What is your vision for your life? What is your true life's purpose? Underneath all the day-to-day routines, what deeply matters to you? What have you always wanted to experience even though it continually eludes you? What are the specific or tangible results you've always wanted to achieve that have stayed beyond your reach? What would life on the Skinny Branches look like for you, and what will it take to fully go for it? What are the steps you've been unwilling to take thus far? And most importantly, *what have you been waiting for?* Life is not a dress rehearsal. Life is now. Life is happening all around us and only in this moment.

For almost three decades, I've been working with people to help them answer these questions for themselves. I've spent my entire adult life training and coaching people, helping them break through their limiting attitudes, beliefs, habits, and ways of being, in order to create their most important visions for life. I've been helping them reinvent and transform their approaches so that they can realize those visions, and ultimately, alter the trajectory of their futures and those of their children. I've trained and coached hundreds of thousands of people, both in large groups and in individual sessions, with an awareness that we all hope our lives will turn out as good as, or better than, our parents' lives did. Similarly, we all want our children to someday be more evolved and turn out better than us. Through a committed and rigorous process of experiential-based exercises and activities, my students and clients come to realize a renewed and genuine vision for their lives and are empowered to change what is necessary to achieve it. Some of the essential ingredients in this formula derive from powerful lessons and experiences I've learned through redesigning my own actions and behaviors. Additionally, through extensive work in developing myself as a transformational trainer and coach, my intention is to pass on and facilitate this process for the maximum number of people possible.

Often, students come into a training session with one of two mindsets. Either they come in thinking they already know everything, or conversely, they come in believing that they don't matter, that they're not worthy, or that they simply won't be able to change their lives no matter what they do. Once they complete the many processes I guide them through, they reach entirely new levels of awareness and empowerment. They understand and believe in themselves in ways they never have before. They develop a new attitude and perspective on life itself and what they are capable of within it. They leave saying things they've never said before with any real conviction: "I can do anything I put my mind to. I am powerful. I now know why I am here. I am bigger than any challenge or life circumstances." Then, they go out and create extraordinary results within their everyday world. Here's a common example of this transformation: Often, people who attend my trainings will reveal that they've been married for twenty-plus years but only remain with their spouse due to a sense of duty and obligation. They are still married because they said, "Till death do us part," at the ceremony, and are now struggling with the fear of what their families or friends might think of them if they break that vow. What's missing is the experience of being "in love," being in a partnership of admiration and respect. I work with these couples to break through their old, tired ways of thinking, to let go of their past, and to change the characterizations they have of one another. In the process, they learn how to identify and give up their negative interpretations and fixed beliefs. They learn how to interrupt unhealthy patterns of behavior that tear away at the fabric of trust and intimacy within their relationship. This work allows them to see each other through a fresh pair of eyes, to experience a clean slate, and to invent a new vision and purpose for being together, one that is expressed through greater understanding and forgiveness—as well as heightened love, passion, and joy.

Throughout this book there are many such stories of the profound transformations of real people who come from all walks of life—people of different ages, backgrounds, and cultural influences, different levels of education and socioeconomic standing, different fundamental beliefs on religion, politics, and society in general—people who on the surface may seem to have little in common except that they possess a vision for creating a happy, healthy, and fulfilling life.

I certainly understand what it means to have such a vision. My life experience might be unique to me, but the essence of it, and the purpose behind it, are not unlike your own. In the first part of this book I will share my story, including the events and experiences that eventually led me to find my way out onto my own Skinny Branches, and I'll describe how those experiences began a three-decade-long journey of standing for over 100,000 people to transform the quality of their own lives. Everything that follows the first chapter is organized like a guide, similar to how a professional coach would guide a client. After establishing a context for personal transformation through my own journey, I will elaborate in great detail on five specific keys to living on the Skinny Branches, which will lead you on your way to creating your own version of a life worth living. These keys include a unique blend of inspiration and practicality—significant new actions to take and unmistakable reasons to take them. These keys can and should be absorbed at your own pace with time built in for practice, trial and error and adjustment, and the lasting experiences that come with new success. Think of this reading process as a marathon with many individual sprints sprinkled throughout. You will experience moments when you urgently want to act on an idea, and other moments that are best reserved for calm self-reflection. One of my favorite quotes comes from the theoretical physicist Albert Einstein: "Life is a gift. And if we agree to accept it, we must contribute in return. When we fail to contribute, we fail to adequately answer why we are here."

So why *are* we here? What *is* our purpose in life? Is it our purpose to do exactly what we are told to do? Is it our purpose to fit in and follow the herd? To go through the motions, acting and reacting without thinking? To simply exist? Is our greatest achievement in life to do just enough to get by? I don't think so. I believe our purpose in life actually begins with discovering what that purpose actually is. We then manifest this purpose by figuring out ways to have a positive effect and permanent impact on others, beginning with the people to whom we are closest in life—our family, friends, colleagues, and community. But all of this is theoretical until we actually create our vision by realizing new experiences and producing unprecedented results, which requires more than mere thoughts and ideas.

By reading this book, you will discover the transformative power of *declaration*. You will learn how to believe in yourself in new ways, as well as believe in your capacity to create results that are consistent with your true purpose. Part of making a declaration is saying, out loud, what we intend to cause. When we don't share our goals out loud, we're not held accountable by anyone to see them through. If we don't say it out loud, we're not truly "at risk." Declaring a goal or mission out loud involves inherent risk because it invites the possibility of failure. By applying the practices presented throughout this journey, you will learn how to get past your fears. You will learn not only that it is possible to transform your relationship with fear, but also that the experience of it can be magical. The first step is to realize that fear is often just a conversation you're having *with* yourself, *about* yourself, in relation to the events and circumstances in the world around you. It is often an interpretation of something that leads to an emotional response and/or a kinesthetic experience. With rare exception (for example, a tiger just showed up and he might be hungry), fear is usually not real and is seldom based on fact. But even if you do encounter a tiger, different people will respond to that situation in very different ways because people have an individual *relationship* with their fears. FEAR can often be thought of as an acronym for False Evidence Appearing Real. It has no real power except the power we give it. When we lose focus of our purpose and of what we thirst for in life, we can easily become puppets to our fear, which only hinders our ability to manifest our purpose.

This book will also give you the opportunity to discover what *really* matters to you—the stuff that lies below the surface. You will gain clarity on your unique vision for anything and everything related to what really matters to you, and you will bring that vision alive and declare it out loud. Many of us have dreams that we keep to ourselves, dreams that we only dare imagine before going to sleep or upon waking up. We think to ourselves about what we really want, about how life could be different, could be better, but we keep these hopes and dreams to ourselves. We don't share them with anyone. In reading this book, you will learn to share your deepest visions, and in the process, instinctively expand on them—giving them shape and making them come alive. You will experience what it means to truly be *vision-driven*.

If you really pay attention to what people are talking about while hanging out at Starbucks or during "happy hour" after work, you will often hear them discussing what is wrong with their lives—who's to blame for their problems, what's *not* working at work and at home, or what's *missing in life*. Women talk to each other about how men are "players" who can't be trusted. Men talk to each other about how women are fake and consumed with how they look. It's a game we buy into and play unconsciously. People say things like, "Life's a bitch and then you marry one." The most common response to such statements is to nod or chuckle in approval. Routine conversations include complaining about how life is tough and relationships are hard: "My wife is so high maintenance. No matter what I do, it's never good enough—she's never happy." Or, "My husband never does his fair share around the house. I wish he would contribute more. He can be so selfish." You hear variations of these same conversations wherever you go. There is plenty of statistical evidence to verify just how much we're drawn towards the problems of the world. If customers are happy with their experiences at a business establishment, they'll typically tell one or two people. But if they are unhappy with their experience, they'll tell a dozen people, with emphasis on just how bad their experience was. Negativity and dissatisfaction spread at a far quicker rate, and much more widely, than positivity and excitement. Think about it. Are you more likely to hear someone say, "She's such a positive person," or "She can be so negative"? Always focusing on the negative is one of the most significant conditioning influences in all of society. When you're driving down the road and there's an accident up ahead on the *other side* of the median, the traffic on your side slows to a crawl. Why? Most of us can't help but slow down, if only for the possibility of witnessing the drama of human suffering.

In today's world of reality television, producers routinely place contestants and participants in situations of extreme stress and pressure with the full intention of capturing people behaving badly. This book is about the opposite of that intention. This book is about realizing a deeply held dream and then creating a life worth living based on your willingness to venture out onto the Skinny Branches while reaching for that dream. This is a process in which you escape your conditioned instincts towards limitation, within yourself as well as among others. You free yourself from the turbulence, stress, and underlying pain and suffering that automatically come with being circumstance-driven or with being focused on the negative. This is a process that allows you to create and inhabit a life you truly want to live, instead of simply standing on the sidelines watching life go by. As previously stated, living on the Skinny Branches will obviously mean different things to different people. You might be a store clerk, a teacher, a manager, a sales person, an entrepreneur who builds a million-dollar business, or something else entirely. No matter what your occupation is, you can either show up to work as an ordinary, run-of-the-mill person, or you can show up as a *master leader*—someone who is vision-driven, positive, and exceptional, someone who lives with integrity and makes decisions that benefit others. The key to success is your attitude and your perspective on your occupation and on life in general. Your title or perceived status is not important. The career itself is incidental to the outcomes generated by the person working the job. Everyone has the capacity to create a life worth living, the capacity to get in touch with a higher purpose and to fulfill that purpose by creating from a place of possibility versus a place of survival, scarcity, or fear.

We live in a world where authenticity is sparse, not valued or fully appreciated. It is a treasured trait when we are children and living a relatively simple existence, but as we get older, our priorities shift. What do we value most as adults? Looking good, being right, and being in control. We operate from unconscious survival mechanisms. As adults, we're concerned and consumed with having all the right answers. As children, we're concerned with nothing except our unquenchable thirst for discovery, with having fun and learning new things. This is why children always ask so many questions. To an adult, knowledge and information are king. To a child, curiosity and creativity are the most important parts of life. If you observe small children in their daily lives, they will often sing and dance for no reason at all. They never just walk through the house. They hop, jump, and skip. They do cartwheels. If they don't know the words to a song, that doesn't stop them from singing. They make up the words—they create. They are always communicating through expressions of happiness, a child's most common state of experience. Children are automatically fulfilled because being fulfilled versus being deficient is not a distinction they have learned *yet*. They don't care how they look or what other people think of them until they learn to care about such things from other people, usually adults. Adults invent so many ways to chip away, both directly and indirectly, at the instinctive and authentic nature of being a child. Ironically, those very same adults often spend a lifetime in search of ways to rekindle their own inner child.

In part, this book is about doing just that—getting back in touch with your true self, that incredibly alive and natural version of yourself. It's about reigniting the unbridled passion, spirit, and joy that is still hidden somewhere inside all of us. Who needs a coffee or an espresso shot every morning? Not a five-year-old. Who cares whether it's Friday or Monday? Again, not children. As adults, we have to schedule recreational activities and vacations—we have to schedule our "joy." We have to create "date night" and schedule intimacy with our spouses. Most of our adult lives are spent in constant activity. We are always doing, working, or planning. Every week we spend forty, fifty, sixty-plus hours of our waking life focused on work-related activities, and for most of us, it's a job we don't even want because we don't genuinely enjoy it. Between our careers, jobs, homes, family responsibilities, and friendships, we become hamsters running around and around on never-ending wheels. We run like banshees on autopilot from one thing to the next—wake up, work, eat, sleep, repeat. In the process, we have learned to settle for mediocrity. We lack awareness when it comes to the creative potential of life itself. We lack appreciation for ourselves and for the people who matter most to us. Life is not meant to be mediocre. It isn't meant to be just "fine" or "okay."

From the moment we're born, life is about living fully expressed, unapologetically passionate about the things that matter to us. If we truly want our dreams to come true, then we must wake up and open our eyes to what we are truly capable of. We must relate differently to whatever stands in our way. So as you begin the journey of this book, ask yourself: "Why am I here? What is my true purpose? Why am I doing what I'm doing? Am I being who I really want to be, or is there something else available for me?" Clarify what you want. Choose what is most important to you. Take the time to stop for a minute, get off the treadmill, turn off autopilot, and take a good, honest look at your life. Take inventory so that you can identify your most deeply held inspirations and aspirations. What will make you genuinely jump out of bed at 6 a.m. because you want to, not because you have to?

Life on the Skinny Branches is about waking up and using your brain, your heart, and your passion, in order to create and design the future you want to live within and live up to. Think of it as the opportunity to design your own ride at Disneyland. Imagine that you only have one ticket and once chance to create that ride, to jump on it and go. You owe it to yourself to make that one experience worth it. Look out toward the Skinny Branches and you'll find what you're looking for. Begin to bridge the gap between what's been missing and what's now possible—having it all.

Chapter One

STARTING AT THE BOTTOM

ALL OF THE WORK I do as a trainer and coach—whether it be with individuals or couples, young, middle-aged, or mature—has been, and still is, unmistakably influenced by my own personal journey of transformation. I was born in Tucson, Arizona in 1964 to Anita and Roger Strasner. I wasn't born into any special privilege, opportunity, or status, and I certainly wasn't a member of a perfect family either. In fact, my parents divorced when I was around a year old. Shortly after the divorce, my mom moved to Los Angeles with my older brother Larry and me, where we lived very close to my grandparents and great-grandparents. When I was four, my mother went to Washington, D.C. for some much-needed breathing room, and to recover from an incredibly painful divorce from my father. During this time, Larry and I lived with my grandparents in Los Angeles. One day, my mother called my brother and me to tell us that she had remarried, that we were going to have a new father, Bob, and that we were moving out to Washington D.C. to live with them. This was a significant memory in my life. I'll never forget the telephone call or the long flight from California to Washington D.C. When my brother and I got off the plane, our mom and "new" dad were both there to greet us. My mother was very emotional and gave both Larry and me big hugs and kisses. I don't recall Bob saying anything significant to us at the airport, so I didn't know what to make of him at first. I only remember him being tall. As Larry and I sat in the backseat of the car on the way home, I recall experiencing a strange, unusual feeling of comfort. During that car ride home, I remember Bob reaching over the back of his seat and handing me a chocolate bar, which I gladly accepted with excitement. It seemed like this was his way of connecting with us.

This first experience of interaction with my new dad ultimately became the norm during my childhood. I recall spending a lot of time with him in my younger years, physically being around him, often working in the yard or around the house, yet I don't recall much intimacy or emotional connection. There was not a lot of physical contact—not a lot of hugging, kissing, or parental affection. Over time, I began to desperately long for these things. But as I grew older and learned more about my new father, I thought the world of him. For me, he was very intelligent, interesting, hardworking, honest, sophisticated, provocative, and often irreverent. I found him to be absolutely fascinating. Additionally, he had a fantastic sense of humor. Being around someone like this made it easy to be in awe. When we first met, my mother told me to call him Dad, so I did. At the time, I didn't really understand what the word meant. But because of how much I admired and ultimately respected him, I felt comfortable calling him Dad, and I still do to this day. When I was four, it was just a word to me, but as I got older, it felt like more of a conscious declaration, an affirmation, to call him Dad. I was no longer simply following my mother's instructions. I *wanted* him to be my dad. I wanted him to think of me as his son, not just his stepson. Why? Because I was looking for love, connection, and a sense of belonging. He had a tremendous influence on me. I learned so many things from him: to appreciate what I have, to investigate, to consider my thoughts, to honor my word, to show respect for others, to articulate my point of view in a clear and intelligent way, to live by my principles, to laugh, to use my mind to create ideas, to realize life isn't always fair, among many other life lessons.

Unfortunately, in large part due to human nature, the experiences that impacted me the most weren't these gifts I received from him, but the profound disappointment I felt in his presence. I became convinced that I wasn't worthy, that I wasn't good enough, and that I would never live up to his expectations. No matter what I did, I never experienced the emotional connection, acceptance, and reassurance I needed. I began to feel tremendous insecurity, and I was convinced I wasn't smart enough, that something was wrong with me.

When my brother Larry and I fought or argued, it seemed like my dad never defended me. When we were given chores, he would just accept it when Larry slacked off. Because my dad wasn't into sports, he basically showed minimal interest in—and very little support for—my love and passion to play. Often, I would reach out for his support when struggling in school, and he would be unavailable or too busy with his own work. When I disagreed with his point of view, he would tell me I was wrong in a very intense and intimidating way. His words would rattle me and shake me to the core. I constantly second-guessed my own thoughts, and then self-doubt would creep in and consume me. I was looking for someone to believe in me, to stand up for me. For years I hoped that person could be him, but too often I was let down. I wanted to feel special and important, like I mattered, but by the time I was in my teens, I was instead feeling angry, lost, insecure, alone, and insignificant.

This leads me to my relationship with mom. My earliest memories and experiences with my mother affected me profoundly, and as a result, our relationship was the most influential and difficult of many in my life. To begin, my mother has many beautiful qualities that make her an incredible person and mother. She is emotionally connected. She always had her hand on the pulse of my feelings and the feelings of everyone in our family. As a child, if I wasn't being my best self, which in hindsight was most of the time, my mother would sit me down for hours in an attempt to support me and do her best to encourage me. She was 100% committed to our happiness, our dreams, our educations, our health, our well-being, and our development as people. On top of that, she gave me a lot of intangible gifts. For example, she was the one who always encouraged me to speak not only from my mind, but also from my heart. She taught me to listen to what people are saying, but also to what they're not saying—the music behind their words. Because of her, I'm in tune with and sensitive to my surroundings. I use these gifts and talents in every area of my life, as a parent and as a husband, and in my profession as a trainer and coach. Another important and amazing quality of my mother is the way she said the words "I love you" thousands of times during my childhood, often accompanied with warm hugs. I appreciate my mother for her contributions to me in these very important ways. However, along with these important, valuable, and meaningful experiences, were other events and moments that caused me tremendous pain and hurt.

Our unique mother-son relationship and my subsequent interpretations of our interactions caused me to develop the most dominating limiting beliefs and views of myself and my place in the world. In addition to all of the amazing qualities my mother had and still has, she also possessed some ways of being that didn't benefit my growth.

As a child, I was convinced that my mother not only favored, but also liked—and even loved—Larry more than me. My mother could be an incredibly dominant, controlling, and sometimes self-centered person. During any conflict I had with my brother, the noise was what bothered her, so she would often scream over it, and her anger always seemed to be directed at me. It didn't matter what had happened or what the cause of the conflict was. In her eyes, Larry was the perfect son, the little prince who could do no wrong. Meanwhile, I was the "difficult child," the court jester, the troublemaker. I was Larry's brother, not my own person. Whether or not my mother actually used these exact words, I constantly heard her voice in my head: "Why can't you be more like Larry? He's so easy." As a child, my feelings about my mother were very extreme, like a scary roller coaster with incredible highs and lows. It was absolutely a love-hate relationship, emphasis on the hate.

Those lows were what impacted me the most. I did not recognize or feel her genuine love for me. Even when she said those words ("I love you") everyday, even when she hugged me, kissed me, showing incredible affection at times—no matter what she said or did, I still didn't believe her words were honest. I just didn't get it. Her behavior was often erratic, and her emotional reactions were unpredictable. She cried a lot. She seemed to be depressed and unhappy, and she fought with her own parents and with my dad, Bob. Behind her back, I used to call her the "wet blanket." I used to say, sarcastically, that if we were having fun of any kind, my mother's job was to extinguish that fun immediately. I often felt that her main motivation in having children was to fill the emptiness, the void, and numb the pain that she was feeling due to what was missing from her own life. I allowed some of the things she said to hurt me deeply, and I used those statements as evidence that something was wrong with me. I heard her say things like, "I gave up my college education and career dreams for you," and "Michael, the reason our friends like you is because they don't know you like I do." She would say, "Michael, I like soccer better than football." Larry, of course, was the star soccer player.

It was not only things she said that wounded me—her actions played a large part, too. On one of my birthdays, my parents went on a vacation, saying they really needed time together to reconnect as a couple. I spent my birthday at a family friend's house. Even though Kris Robison did her best to make the day special, I felt completely worthless and unloved. Would they have left on vacation during Larry's birthday? No way.

One Christmas morning, my siblings and I went downstairs to see what Santa brought us, and while Larry and my sister Danielle got everything they wanted, I received only a couple of small things. I said to Larry, "Looks like slim pickings this year, I'm going back to sleep." What actually happened was that my parents had forgotten to place my gifts under the tree, but at the time, I just saw more evidence that I was less important than my siblings. I can't recall an instance when Larry was without proper clothes and sneakers while I would mostly get his hand-me-downs. In a number of instances, I wore sneakers with holes in them for long periods of time. I know my father was working hard and dedicated to doing everything he could to support us as a family. Clearly, we didn't have a lot of money and the budget was tight, but it seemed as if Larry's needs were squeezed onto my mother's priority list, with no room for my own. She would rarely take us to any practices or games, to the movies or the mall, or to go see friends. She only came to see me play at my various sporting events on a few occasions. This was very disappointing to me and over time I built up tremendous resentment and bitterness towards her. My trust issues only grew worse. Saying "I love you" every day doesn't hold any power if it isn't accompanied by consistent, corresponding actions.

Given that education and learning was the top priority for my parents, we usually participated in activities that were more enjoyable for adults than children, such as going to art exhibits, festivals, and museums. This was, of course, a major priority for them. At the time, it was not my top priority at all. I had a passion and love for sports, and I wished they could not only understand it, but also get behind it. For the most part, they didn't. Instead, I felt like I had no vote, no power, no value. I felt like I didn't belong in my family. I was the black sheep. I didn't fit in. I often found myself alone in my room, feeling lost and confused. At some point, I invented the explanation that my mother had never been in love with my biological father, Roger, and that she had only given birth to me out of a sense of duty and obligation. In the early 1960s, abortion wasn't an option, but I certainly felt that if it were more socially acceptable, given the marital problems my parents were having, it could have been a perfect justification. Given my mother's emotional state during her pregnancy with me, a radical reaction could have easily been a conscious or subconscious way of dealing with the stress. However, at the time of my youth, I didn't care much about her side of the story, about her point-of-view on anything, or about what she was feeling. All I was concerned with was what I was going through. I constructed walls of armor and steel to bury my true gifts and genuine talents under the avalanche of victim conversations that consumed me.

Larry and I were raised by my mother and stepfather, but we also had a relationship with Roger, our biological father. It was a challenging relationship for me, to say the least. My early childhood memories of him are spotty. However, many of the memories I do have are fantastic, full of fun and excitement—playing catch with him, participating in various sporting activities, bodysurfing, hanging out at the beach, and basking in the sun. But Roger, my father, was like a magician with a disappearing act: *Now you see him, now you don't.* Larry and I would only get to visit him every two years in San Diego, where he was living with his new wife, Mickey. While we were together, he acted like a totally normal dad. He was very involved, cared about the things I cared about, asked hundreds of questions, and he seemed to really listen to, and care about, what I had to say. Because it was summer, we did all the things any boy would love to do, especially with his father. But the inconsistency of the relationship had a tremendous impact on Larry and me. As time went on, the relationship became a constant source of disappointment. We would spend five or six weeks of quality father-son time together during those summer trips. In that period of time, I even felt wanted, important, and connected. And then suddenly, it would be over, and those warm thoughts and feelings would vanish. Afterwards, there would be one or two telephone calls per year, maybe on my birthday. He would occasionally send letters, but beyond that, there was no other contact. It was almost like a dream; it didn't feel real.

Our relationship felt very hot-and-cold. After each trip, when I left San Diego to return home, I would go from feeling satiated with a strong sense of belonging, to feeling sadness and emptiness. As I got older, I began to wonder what it would be like to live with him. Would he even want me? Would it be possible? I also thought about how moving across the country to live with my dad might affect my mother and stepfather. Sometimes, the comfort of the known outweighs the discomfort of the unknown, even if we aren't happy with the known and it hasn't led us to what we want. I was experiencing a significant amount of ambivalence. I felt like I was sinking in quicksand, desperately looking for a vine to cling on too. I was longing for some form of stability or platform to stand on—a sense of security.

When Larry and I first moved to the East Coast, we lived in Washington, D.C. with our mother and stepfather. We moved around a lot and lived in several places during those early years as a new family: D.C., Virginia, and New Jersey. They were all short-term, transient places—not real homes. While in Virginia, my sister Danielle was born, and sometime afterwards, we ended up moving to a town just outside of Boston called Natick, which I considered our first real home. It was during these formative years that I began to develop my emotional insecurities and disempowering interpretations of life and my life events.

In addition to my relationships with my mother and both of my fathers, I had a significant and challenging relationship with my brother Larry. During my childhood, my brother and I were virtually inseparable. We did almost everything together until I was about fifteen years old. During just about every major influential event and moment of significance, Larry was there. He is a year older than I am, and back then he was the "prince," the one who was perfect and, of course, always right. We were extremely competitive with each other, but I usually felt like the runner-up, as if people thought of me as "Larry's brother" and never the other way around. I was never *me*. Everything I ever did was measured against what my brother had already done. We were both very stubborn, and we each had strong views on what we should do; where we should go; what sports, activities, or games we should play; what the rules would be; and how we would determine the winner. Most of the time, we would be so excited and focused on what we were doing, it would appear as though we were actually very close and getting along. But then, something would always happen: I would make a mistake and he would jump all over me; I would beat him at a game, and he would get angry and become a poor sport; I would overreact to a rules violation; he would instigate a confrontation with me because he was bored; I would be jealous of his relationship with our mother and start criticizing him; or I would want to play a game that he didn't want to play, and then annoy him until he agreed. For us, that was the way we related to each other.

Whenever I had a conflict with my parents, which was often, I would look for support from my brother, and most of the time, he took their side. Even if he didn't have all the information, he just assumed that it must be my fault, that my issues had caused the problem. To Larry, I was always wrong. The issue would then escalate into a conflict between the two of us, and sometimes the confrontation got physical. Larry was very strong. I couldn't contend with him on a physical level, so I would fight back with words. Things would only get worse, and then there would be an intervention from my parents, which always led to even bigger trouble for me. Adding up all the days I was grounded as a child, it felt like a lifetime, and it seemed like nothing ever got resolved. The most I could ever hope for was neutrality. I longed for a cease-fire, knowing that the war would always begin again tomorrow.

There were a myriad of reasons for me to give in and simply resign myself to a life of mediocrity, playing small and selling out to playing a background role in life. The perceived greatness of my brother cast a large shadow from which I saw no escape. There seemed to be no possibility for me to shine. In a perfect world, there would have been enough room for both of us, but I had decided that it was either him or me, and Larry always won. Even though I saw myself as a victim in my relationship with my brother, I was in no way innocent. I contributed my fair share of annoyance, irritation, and frustration to him as well. I was completely and pathetically jealous of him on many levels. He was handsome, likable, and confident. He knew when to shut up and follow the rules, and when to speak up. He was close to and connected with my mother, and basically everything just seemed to flow so easily and effortlessly for him. On the other hand, I had already made up my mind that nothing was easy. I was constantly undermining and sabotaging myself, both consciously and unconsciously. I would begin arguments and conflicts with Larry just to provoke him. Often, I would take out my frustrations of my own shortcomings or breakdowns and project them onto my mom and dad. My need to be right about how "wrong" they were or how "wronged" I was, wasn't enough for me. I would take it as far as possible and make things worse. Given my disempowered view of myself and my complete inability to minimize the damage or resolve any issues, I always turned a minor problem into a catastrophe with ease and efficiency. I was a glutton for punishment. These relationships had the greatest impact in shaping my experience of myself, my place in our family, my participation in school, my perceived social status, and ultimately, my view of the world. Ironically, without my own belief, acceptance, and confidence, I also seemed to have a lot going for me. Others recognized my gifts and talents, but at that time, any and all positive feedback or results had minimal influence in my overall perception of myself. For me, compliments went in one ear and out the other. Anything positive was fleeting and had absolutely zero sustainability.

For example, I was an excellent athlete. I played virtually every sport—including football, baseball, basketball, hockey, tennis, track, and golf—at a high level and learned each game very quickly. Ultimately, the game I really excelled at was golf. When I was thirteen, I picked up the game from watching it on TV. It seemed like a very challenging game, which is part of the reason I was drawn to it. Given my limited physical size, it was also a game I could play without the risk of injury, unlike the other sports I enjoyed. I taught myself how to play golf and received no lessons. Within two years, I made the high school golf team and moved my way up from tenth to fourth to first on a team of twelve. I was undefeated in my individual matches in my junior and senior years, with a record of 15-0-1. Once, in a practice round, I got a hole-in-one on the third hole at Putterham Meadows Golf Club, in Brookline, Mass. I made it in front of my teammates and our coach. In addition to being on the Brookline Varsity Golf team, I was also selected to the All-Conference Team by the league coaches and was invited to play in the Massachusetts All-State Tournament. Sounds great, right? I should have been on top of the world, but I wasn't. These results still weren't enough to interrupt my thoughts of unworthiness, insecurity, and self-doubt.

In school, most of my teachers thought that I was intelligent, bright, and talented. They would tell me how much they enjoyed having me in class, how they appreciated my contribution to class projects, and that my potential was limitless. My performance in school completely mirrored my experience of myself and my life. Essentially, I would do just enough to get by. I hardly ever put in 100% effort to complete my work with excellence. I often sat in class daydreaming of a life somewhere far away from the miserable feeling, the emptiness, the overwhelming sense that my life was irrelevant to anyone. Every once in a while, when I really got into a subject or topic, it would come easily to me and I'd earn an excellent grade. With minimal studying, I'd pull it off. My teacher would congratulate me and say how proud they were, and it basically meant nothing to me. Why? Because I knew what I had done to get the grade, which was usually not much. I knew the positive feedback wasn't really earned, so it had no impact. My lack of genuine effort only reinforced my feelings about myself, and when I would get an acknowledgment from my teachers or my mother or father, it felt hollow because I knew the truth. Even though I felt unworthy, I would still look for recognition and acknowledgment in any way I could get it, hoping it would one day make a difference.

I have two sisters: Danielle, who is five years younger than me, and Candide, who is twelve years younger. They were both conceived by my mom and my dad, Bob. I also have a brother, Andy, who is ten years younger, and a sister, Missy, who is fourteen years younger. They both come from my father, Roger, and his second marriage to Mickey.

Because we were raised by my mother and stepfather, I became very close with Danielle and Candide. Technically they are my half-sisters, but not in spirit or in my life experience with them. I was there when they were born, and they have always been my true sisters. They are both absolutely beautiful human beings in all ways.

Danielle was the sweetest, kindest, and most thoughtful sibling—straight out of the mold of goodness that we all aspire to be in our lives. When I needed a hug or needed to feel any sense of belonging, I would go directly to Danielle and she would always accept me and love me without judgment. Candide was full of joy, smiles, and abundantly playful energy. I often picked her up from school, and it was always a privilege, not a burden. She would entertain me with her songs, dancing, humor, and infectious spirit.

My sisters lifted me up and made my existence tolerable, and I felt special with them, even if the feeling was only temporary. Back then, I actually fabricated the idea that the reason they loved me so much, and thought I was such a great brother, was because they were much younger and couldn't be influenced by what Larry and my parents thought.

Because I wasn't raised under the same roof as my other half-siblings, Andy and Missy, I missed years of opportunities to get to know them and develop the same level of significance in our relationships during childhood. In our adult years, of course, we have become very close and they are my brother and sister.

However, during our childhood visits every couple of years, my half-siblings and I shared lots of fun, exciting, and adventurous moments. It wasn't easy to see the way Andy and Missy lived, the quality of life they received, and the abundant opportunities they enjoyed. Most importantly, it was difficult knowing that they got to be with my dad full-time. This inequity produced some anger, resentment, and tension for both Larry and me as children. The theme song from a popular TV show at the time, *The Jeffersons*, comes to mind: "…We're moving on up, to the east side, to the deluxe apartment in the sky…we finally got a piece of the pie!" The only problem was that Larry and I got a very small slice of the pie, and it came in a to-go box. Larry and I were anything but spoiled, but visiting our dad would produce a lot of conversations about the unfairness of the situation: "What did we do wrong? Why not us?" We experienced feelings of entitlement and resentment.

Of course, we took a lot of our frustrations out on each other, and on Andy, who I'd given the title, "West Coast Prince." For

Larry, there was only room for one prince, and Andy was moving in on his turf and threatening his self-appointed domain of dominance and authority. For me, I was the second-oldest among the five of us, so Andy being older than Missy meant absolutely nothing to me. He was another prince who needed to be demoted by any means necessary. I saw it as survival of the fittest.

Andy was smart, witty, and athletic. He worshipped Larry and me. Was he spoiled? Yes. But he didn't deserve to be treated the way he was by us. We were simply jealous and were taking it out on him. Missy, however, was in the same category as my other sisters: sweet, adorable, and absolutely accepting of me and everyone. But because we didn't grow up together, and there was such a large age gap, I felt more like an uncle or a cousin to her. We had a connection, but it was a distant one.

As I mentioned earlier, my dad, Bob, gradually became a very influential figure in my life. He was incredibly smart and worldly, and was knowledgeable on a wide range of subjects: politics, science, sociology, culture, and more. He was so fascinated with life and the world in general. He would engage me in conversations about current events, from politics and political leaders to social justice, and most importantly, about what I wanted to do with my life. These conversations were often challenging, even difficult. It wasn't easy to respond while I was just in search of something reasonably intelligent to say. I always believed that no matter what I said, it wouldn't be good enough, or that he wouldn't quite get it. I even feared that he would tear my ideas apart, that he would dismiss my dreams as unrealistic fantasies. My insecurities were heightened by my need for his acceptance and approval.

Of course, like any child, I had many thoughts and dreams about my future. I wanted to be a professional athlete, a lawyer, an actor, a singer in a rock-n-roll band, a stand-up comedian, and someday, I hoped to maybe get into politics. As my father challenged my thoughts in search of my motives, my level of commitment, and my plan of action to achieve any of these dreams, my feelings of unworthiness would take over. By the end of these conversations—even though it wasn't his intention—I firmly believed I couldn't succeed and I didn't have what it took. I actually remember saying to myself, "Maybe someday I'll find the confidence I need to go after what I want…I hope." I couldn't express these true feelings and thoughts to him because it would have required vulnerability from me, and by my teenage years, I had already started to shut down my real self from the outside world. In my eyes, my own family, including the home I lived in, was part of that outside world. I was barricading myself behind the walls I'd put up.

When I turned fifteen, a few significant, life-defining events occurred. One day, while doing chores around the house, I found a will. I had no idea what it was until I carefully opened the envelope. On the page, I clearly saw Larry's name (of course) in several locations, along with the names of my sisters, Danielle and Candide. My name, however, was nowhere to be found. Not seeing my name on that document was a traumatic experience for me. From my perspective, that omission from the will only confirmed everything about myself and my family that I thought to be true. It confirmed that I was not loved in the same way my brother and sisters were, that I didn't fit in, that I was the black sheep in the family, and not in the ways that someone with such a label can be admired.

As I mentioned earlier, Larry and I would see our father, Roger, about once every two years, and in between those visits, he would occasionally write us these long, ten-page letters. They were letters of substance from a father who actually seemed to care about me and my life. In no way were they written out of obligation. Sometimes I would reread the letters four or five times just to feel connected to him in those moments. Not long after the difficult experience of finding myself omitted from the will, I went to visit him alone for the first time. While I was in San Diego, I felt a sense of confidence I had never felt before. I think this was at least partially because I went without Larry, so there was no competition for love, time, or attention. It was an amazing experience, and I didn't want it to end. It was the shot in the arm I was looking for—it was what I needed in order to see hope in changing my perceptions and feelings about myself and my future.

When I returned to Boston after the summer, my mother picked me up at the airport. She was, as usual, very perceptive in her connection to my state of mind. She noticed how excited I was and could see the spark in my eyes while I described my summer experiences. She looked at me and said, "Would you like to go live with your father permanently?" Even though I was terrified, I took a risk and said yes. I had thought about the possibility all summer but doubted if I would ever get the chance, or if it was even a realistic possibility. When my mother asked, it was easy to see how difficult this would be for her. She was crying, but for the first time, I really felt she was considering what course of action would give me the best opportunity to succeed. I appreciated that she was putting aside her own sadness, disappointment, or maybe even feelings of failure, to support me in the best way she could. She gave me the permission to call my dad and ask.

When I called to express my desire to live with him, my heart felt like it was going to jump out of my chest. I was shaking, scared, and I felt very vulnerable. I was crying, because in that moment, I had never wanted anything from anyone more than I wanted to hear him say yes. In my fifteen years of life up to that point, this was the first time I had ever really asked him for anything. It was the single biggest risk I had ever taken. His immediate response was one of excitement and joy, and everything he said made me think that he was going to say yes. He asked to talk it over with his wife, Mickey, and said he would call me the following day. When I hung up the phone, I remember feeling confident and certain of the answer I would receive. My thoughts swirled: *He wants it just as much as I do, doesn't he? He'll convince Mickey, won't he? Andy and Missy would want me to live with them and be part of their family too, wouldn't they? It's about time my dad stepped up for his son, after missing fifteen years, yes?* The next day, I received the call. He told me that he had discussed it with Mickey and the answer was unfortunately no, and that he was sorry. I don't remember much about the rest of the conversation, but I know I was stunned, shocked, and hurt. He said something about how hard it would be on my mom, and I just remember the sinking feeling in my gut. The main thing I heard after that was, *blah... blah... blah...* End of call. End of the hope I had of something changing in my life. When my dad said no, it felt like a piece of me died. I was throwing out an SOS, and he hadn't heard my call. I told myself I would never ask him or anybody else for anything ever again. I would never allow myself to be that vulnerable and exposed. This incident with my father was just one more piece of evidence that reinforced all of my existing limiting beliefs and interpretations.

Around that time, something else happened at school that had a huge impact on me. During French class one day, my teacher was giving a friend of mine a hard time. After she'd walked away, I whispered to him, "Don't worry about it, David. She's a bitch." I didn't mean for her to hear me. I was just trying to stick up for my friend. Later that day, I was on the phone in my room when I heard a knock at the door. It was my dad, Bob. He never came to my room, so right away I knew something was up. When I opened the door, his face was bright red. He looked at me sternly and said, "Did you call your French teacher a bitch?" My initial thought was: *How could he possibly know this?* I really didn't think anyone but David had heard me. My dad didn't give me a chance to explain myself. He confronted me in a very harsh way, so harsh it rocked me to the core. It seemed that no matter what I did, everything always backfired, either by my own doing or in my interpretations of others' actions. When he confronted me, I decided that this was the last straw. I ended up running away from home for three days. At fifteen, I firmly believed that I couldn't trust "these" people. I couldn't trust my own family. I thought that they didn't care about me or about my life. They didn't know who I was, didn't understand me or value what was important to me, so I completely shut down and decided to get out and get as far away as possible.

I turned into a complete rebel with a giant chip on my shoulder. I was committed to going against the grain. I promised myself I would go to college as far away from my family as possible. I decided that Jacksonville University in Florida would be my destination. It was my best option to get as far away from Boston as I could, and to continue playing golf. (I'd created a fantasy in my mind that if I had the opportunity to practice year-round, maybe I'd have the chance to be a professional golfer someday.) Distance, both physical and emotional, became my creed. When my parents found out, they crunched the numbers and told me we couldn't afford it. I thought to myself sarcastically: *Wow, now there's a shock!* Of course my parents couldn't afford to send me to the school of my choosing. I had to settle for a lesser one. I wasn't Larry, who of course got to go to his dream school.

In the end, I selected a small college called Georgia Southern University, which was still plenty far away. My parents warned me that I wouldn't like the South, but I didn't listen. I was now firmly set in my belief that they didn't care about me, and I was going to do what I needed to do and go where I needed to go. I was angry and bitter. I was playing the victim. They had a lot of concerns about me going to a small school in Georgia, and because of my view of myself and of them, I couldn't and wouldn't listen. All of their fears and warnings turned out to be 100% accurate. The year I spent in college at GSU was the most traumatizing wake-up call of my life. The realities of the issues people were experiencing in the world at large—as well as in the United States—hit me like a two-by-four between the eyes. Sexism and racism were rampant. I heard the N-word multiple times a day, and even though it was

1982, it seemed as though not much progress had been made in the South in the past couple decades, at least based on what I'd read in the history books. Even my psychology professor told our class, in response to a student asking about living in the southern U.S., "Just once, I'd like get out of the 18th century and live in the 20th." In a class of 500 students, I seemed to be the only one who realized it was a direct insult to the slow progress being made there, and I felt uncomfortable.

During this time, music was a very important part of my life. The messages in the lyrics of my favorite songs often allowed me to transport myself from where I was to future, faraway dreamlands. To fantasize about what could be, maybe, someday. John Lennon was one of my musical and life heroes. He wrote about peace, honesty, and equality on Earth—a representation of a welcoming, perfect world that was waiting for me away from the suffocating place I had come from. Bob Marley was another powerful and influential voice. His messages about standing up for your rights, about one love and the creation of a new civilization, all spoke to the essence of who I really was inside and what I wanted my life to be about. Music allowed me to escape, even if only temporarily, the life I was living—if you could call it living. I felt completely alone and separate at school in Georgia, still experiencing the same confusion, lack of belonging, and suffocation that I'd felt at home, only now it was even worse. "Should I stay or should I go?" the Clash asked over the airwaves, and I was posing the same question to myself. I thought, *I can't stay at this school, here in Georgia—* staying clearly wasn't working. But I couldn't go back home to Massachusetts because of what that place had come to represent for me. I was damned if I do and damned if I don't. Sitting in a field near the campus, I contemplated these thoughts and feelings and imagined the world caving in on me. I was lost with no direction and no real place to call home. Ultimately, I left Georgia knowing I would never return, knowing that I'd do my best to erase those memories from my mind, like a stain on my windshield to be wiped clean.

After a brief return to Boston, I decided to head to San Diego. This time, I didn't do it to be with my father. I did it in hopes of finding myself and reclaiming the magic of my previous trip. I have always found being in and around the ocean to be refreshing and cleansing, and boy, did I need it then! One night in San Diego, I was out with friends at a college party when I met a girl named Lisa. Instantaneously, for the first time in my life, I fell head over heels in love. Lisa was a student at San Diego State and had been born and raised in Los Angeles. During our relationship, we spent a lot of time traveling back and forth between San Diego and L.A. Her family accepted me with open arms. It was strangely comfortable. Here I was with people I just met, and I somehow felt a strange sense of connection and belonging. Lisa's mother, Carolyn, and I developed a very close and intense relationship. She was a therapist, and I was the perfect person for her to practice therapy on. With so many issues to choose from, I was a menu of opportunities for her to perfect and develop her coaching skills. I was also very perceptive and intuitive myself. I could read people very well—a trait I'd learned from my mother. I used this ability to return the favor with Carolyn. I gave her plenty of valuable feedback, coaching, and support. It was a two-way street. This was the first time I wondered to myself: *Hmmm, maybe I could be a therapist? Maybe I could make a difference in people's lives? Maybe that's my true calling?*

When I was twenty-one years old, living with Lisa and her mother in Los Angeles, Lisa asked me if I would like to attend a special graduation for a personal effectiveness workshop her friend Joelle was completing. I said yes, but only because I knew it would make Lisa happy. The company behind the workshop was called Lifespring. At the time, I'd never heard of it. I didn't even know anything like that existed. I had no way of knowing how much my life would change just because I decided to go.

The graduation was taking place at the Ambassador Hotel, which I knew was the location where Robert Kennedy had been assassinated back in 1968. The graduation event was packed with at least 1,500 guests. Everyone was so excited, bursting with anticipation to enter the main ballroom. The only time I had ever experienced anything like it was at a rock concert. I distinctly remember walking into the room, where the lights were dimmed but not off, and hearing John Lennon's song "Imagine" playing. I was completely overwhelmed with emotions. As the graduation began, I saw men hugging each other, friends and family celebrating, people allowing themselves to be vulnerable and authentic, people expressing sincere feelings of gratitude and love, all while the lyrics from "Imagine" were playing in the background. This was my all-time favorite song. The words meant so much to me that the lyrics, "You may say I'm a dreamer, but I'm not the only one," even appear under my picture in my high school yearbook. While standing at the graduation, I couldn't believe what I was witnessing or experiencing. I felt a deep sense of emotion and an overwhelming feeling of vulnerability. So much so, that I was actually choking on my tears. Because I'd never experienced anything like this before, I didn't think I could handle it. Not wanting anyone to see me cry, I had to keep my composure and control. I quickly rushed out of the room into the hotel lobby, looking for space to breathe. I was hoping no one would see me like this. Why? I was certain that if anyone saw me in this vulnerable state, they would judge me and subsequently reject me. No one had understood me up until that moment, why would they understand me now? Or at least, that was what I thought.

Clearly, something incredible was happening for the people who participated in the workshop, and I badly wanted it for myself but couldn't allow myself to believe it was possible. At the time, my feelings were too difficult to comprehend, I was overwhelmed, and it was hard to talk to Lisa or to anyone else. When the graduation was over, Lisa came out of the building bursting with excitement for her friend Joelle. She was so excited that she told me she was going to the next workshop and that maybe we could do it together. Trying to play it cool, pretending I was only mildly affected, I was too afraid to admit that I desperately wanted to go. I was covering up my true feelings and found myself saying that she should go to the workshop, saying arrogantly that she clearly needed it. The conversation did not go the way I'd envisioned. As usual, I sabotaged myself, and sadly hurt both her and us in the process. Lisa went to the next workshop without me and emerged completely transformed, like I had never seen her before. She went from being shy, insecure, and fearful, to being a person who took risks, spoke up, owned her voice. What a fool I was. It was more important for me to look cool and act arrogant than it was for me to go to the workshop with Lisa and have the same type of profound breakthrough experience for myself. Another opportunity was lost.

Finally, in March of 1986, I took the first step in beginning my personal transformation: I entered the introductory workshop, called the Basic Training, with Lifespring. Even though my first workshop began on that Wednesday evening in March, my journey really began the night I attended Joelle's graduation with my girlfriend Lisa. At the graduation, I started the process of connecting with the life I truly wanted, by first discovering and uncovering what was preventing me from having it. I remember the first night of the training vividly. My trainer's name was Jack. He was powerful, intelligent, and captivating. Right from the start of the workshop, he was challenging us with thought-provoking questions. We were asking ourselves: *What is my vision? What is my purpose in life? What is stopping me? What am I allowing myself to think is more important than having what I want? What is getting in my way? What is holding me back? What are my interpretations? What are my beliefs? What are my rackets? What are my payoffs? What price am I paying? What price are other people in my life paying?*

This was like participating in an interactive and highly relevant philosophy and psychology class that wasn't abstract and general about the world, about being a human being, about society or men and women in their culturally acceptable roles, about theories or concepts, etc. IT WAS ABOUT ME, MICHAEL STRASNER. The other people around me were experiencing the same epiphanies about themselves.

This first training lasted for five days, and it was the first part of a three-part training process, a journey that was approximately four months long. I began to realize—even though I still couldn't fully understand or comprehend the magnitude of impact that Jack would make in my life—that I wanted to have the same skills he did. I wanted to have the distinctions, the ways of being, and the capacity to understand people and learn how to coach and empower them myself.

The Lifespring trainings were, and still remain, the single most profound, extraordinary, and life-altering experiences I have ever had in my life. Period. Up until then, I had been on a one-way street, destined for a life of unfulfilled promise and a legacy of regret and disappointment. Take a moment to consider the beliefs I had made up about myself from my past. Consider the interpretations I had invented and how they affected my place in the world. What else could have possibly happened if I hadn't changed the direction I was taking in my life? Einstein is often credited with saying, "Insanity is doing the same thing over and over again, and expecting different results." I'm not saying that I was insane, but if you stop to think about it, we are only given this one life to live. How could we possibly settle for being a nameless face, an insignificant, second-rate clod of skin and bones?

I interrupted my automatic pilot, my beliefs, and my limiting conversations, ultimately transforming myself during the training process. Through exercises, games, activities, and interactions with fellow students, as well as through the coaching of the trainers, I created a complete breakthrough for myself. The training gave me the opportunity to open my eyes and see how I was living my life. It gave me the opportunity to be completely honest, genuine, and vulnerable about what was driving my actions. I got to the heart of the matter, the source of my pain and unnecessary suffering. To let go and release the hold it had on me. In other words, I consciously woke up from my slumbering existence. I could see clearly for the first time. I realized there was no way I could waste another moment of my life living this way. Not another day. I was sick and utterly exhausted with my victim stories. I was withering away believing I was insecure, small, and inadequate. I couldn't be "Larry's brother" anymore. Instead, it was time for me to become the captain of my ship, the leader of my life, the author of my future. I didn't want to do it because it was what my parents wanted, or because it was what I was "supposed" to do. I wanted to do it for me. It was time to reclaim my gifts, my inner authentic self. I wanted to take back the talents I'd buried under the avalanche of my past experiences and interpretations.

I began to see a vision of what was possible, both in that moment in time, and in the future. I declared myself to be a leader in the world, someone who would use his power and his passion to make a real difference in people's lives. To stand as a leader in a world full of challenges, and to become someone who could be part of the solution, who could maybe even create solutions. I imagined uniting and bringing people together. I committed to creating transformation in and for my family, to heal the wounds for all of us. To let go of our historical family issues and create a new environment, new relationships, and a new way of relating with each other. I wanted this not just for my own family, but for all the families in the world who struggled the way mine did.

With clarity about my personal vision, my career path was obvious. I wanted to do what Jack did; I wanted to be a transformational trainer and coach. It was not another pipe dream or fantasy. It was a legitimate career path, not merely a way for me to make a living or make a difference. I saw it as the most powerful and impactful way to manifest my vision for people. I was moved to make a profound difference in the maximum number of people's lives, immediately. As I began to develop myself as a leader, I received reassuring feedback that I was on the track to success. Constantly and consistently, I heard people say things like, "Michael, you definitely have the tickets needed to be a trainer. You're a great coach. You have transformed my life. Thank you for giving me the tools to break through my fears and limitations." At first, I was overwhelmed with the feedback. I wasn't used to hearing so many positive comments. I kept looking over my shoulder for Larry, to see if they were talking to him or someone else, but they really were saying all of these things to *me*. The momentum was building in the results I was producing with others and in my own experience within myself. The results I was creating in my life were a reflection of my transformation.

For as long as I could remember, I had been drawn to significant leaders, historical figures, inventors, philosophers, artists, and people of all types—Martin Luther King Jr., John F. Kennedy, Gandhi, Amelia Earhart, Thomas Edison, Rosa Parks, Pablo Picasso, Michelangelo, Mother Teresa, John Lennon, and many others. Even today, I look to these people for inspiration and to enhance my views as I seek to understand their lasting contributions to the world. The idea that we, the human race and all living creatures, could somehow all be connected—it fascinates me. Through a synergetic process or a critical mass, I believe that eventually, maybe enough people will transform. The theory of critical mass states that when there is an amount sufficient enough to have a significant effect, then maybe the community or civilization will follow. My vision is to create critical mass in the world so that it becomes abundant, peaceful, loving, and unified. Who knows? Maybe someday, I could be the person mentioned by others as a historical figure who lived his life serving and giving to others, someone who ultimately left a worthy legacy. This was my epiphany.

During my transformation, when I had let go of my past limiting beliefs and limiting interpretations, and redesigned my view of myself and the world around me, the first people I called were my parents. I opened my heart to my mother. Not only did I say the words "I love you," but I also felt genuine love for her for the first time in my life. I forgave her for the things she did, the things she didn't do, the things she said, the things she didn't say, and all the ways I perceived she'd hurt me as a child. I made a commitment to develop a "ten" relationship with her from that moment on. I was talking about creating the highest-level of relationship I could imagine having with my mother, and I meant it. I had never spoken with her this way before, and we were both crying over the phone as I said the words. We both admitted that this was the kind of relationship we'd always wanted. I apologized for all of the horrible things I had said in the past, both to her and about her. I apologized for my lack of appreciation for all she had given me, for showing the whole family love, genuine love, in the best way she knew how. I realized she never meant to hurt me; she didn't have a mean bone in her body. I realized that she was handcuffed by the limitations of her own past experiences with her family and her childhood, just as I had been. It is truly amazing what can happen when we take a risk with other people, when we're willing to be honest and vulnerable with them. It's unbelievable how often the other person will respond in the exact same way. Instead of hurling insults at each other, my mother and I were actually communicating. We were being real with one another. The biggest breakthrough I had was in taking full responsibility for myself. I realized that I filtered everything my mother said through my own experiences and interpretations, and I actually had the choice to hear her words in any way I wanted. The power of taking responsibility for our choices leads us to freedom. I was no longer a victim of my past. I was completely responsible for it.

The result was opening up the space for my mother to claim her own responsibility and forgive not only me, but herself as well. I even addressed the will I'd found all those years ago. Not only did I forgive her for leaving me out, but I told her that I understood why she had done it. Even I would have left myself off the will, given the way I had treated her when I was younger. But then, my mother said something that surprised me—she denied that there ever was a will. Perplexed, I told her where I'd found the document and gave her instructions on how to locate the infamous will. She went to get it, and when she read it to me, all I could do was laugh. *It wasn't a will at all.* It was a document my mother and stepfather had once written indicating what to do with my younger sisters if my parents perished on a trip they were planning to take. Larry would've been responsible for Danielle, while Candide would've lived with my aunt and uncle until she was eighteen. That's all it was. This whole incident serves as a perfect example of the power of INTERPRETATION. When I first read that letter at the age of fifteen, I'd already been firmly convinced that I was unloved, that I was the worthless black sheep of our family, so *of course* I would immediately interpret this simple, innocuous document as a will. When I finally discovered the truth, it was easy to laugh at myself and my ego. I shook my head knowing how many years of unnecessary suffering I had put myself and my parents through. I apologized and asked her to forgive me for the narrative I'd fabricated in my head, and she did. She was completely stunned with my mature behavior and my new attitude and perspective on life. Clean slate, clean space. From there, I enrolled her in my vision for me, for her, and for our whole family. She was even ready to transform herself the same way I had.

After that, I had the courage to talk with my dad, Bob. I told him the same things I'd told her. I told him that I was committed to having an honest and intimate relationship with him—one where we could hug each other and say "I love you" to one another. It felt so good to be the one to take the lead in opening our hearts. It was something I'd always wanted, and deep down inside, I knew he did, too. I also let him know that I was committed to getting my life and my vision for my future straightened out, to live my life in excellence, and to honor my word from this moment forward. In short, I was committed to making him proud of me. Even if he had said no, even if he rejected me again like I'd interpreted him doing for so many years, the fact that I had the courage to declare it was a huge step forward. I remember him responding in an empathetic but more neutral way, probably both hopeful and skeptical of my vision. I didn't have a good track record for credibility, either with him or in my life in general. Having broken my word so often, not sticking to my plans, jumping around from one thing to the next, I understood his reluctance to take what I was saying to him at face value. I acknowledged that he had no reason to believe me based on my past performance, but that this was a new moment and he would soon see that my actions and my behaviors were congruent. Part of my transformation was taking ownership of my results, my mistakes, and cleaning up unresolved broken agreements. He wanted to trust what I was saying, but he needed to see it before he could truly believe it.

If you're reading this right now, and my story hits close to home because you know you're in a similar situation, my hope is that you will find the courage to take a similar risk and call that parent or that other family member with whom you've never had, but always wanted, a genuine connection. If you've never felt that affection from your mother or father, never had parents hold you in their arms and tell you how much they love you, you owe it to yourself to take a chance and let them know how you feel. If they are still alive in this world, then it's not too late.

Ultimately, there were many steps along my transformational journey that allowed me to deal with my past. Not only did I reconcile and resolve the issues with my father, Roger, but since I transformed myself, we have developed a deep love, appreciation and understanding for one another. His level of interest, care and involvement in my life has been consistent and something I always wanted. Through my willingness to let go of my perception of "what happened," I have been able to use my power and confidence to forge and invent an "essential relationship" with him. Now, I can celebrate all of the beautiful gifts he has to offer; his wonderful sense of humor, acceptance of all kinds of people, easy going nature, youthful spirit and incredible sense of adventure.

Regarding the emotionally charged events and examples I mentioned earlier from my childhood. I am completely clear that there are many sides and many interpretations involving every situation. If I were to survey my parents and siblings regarding their recollection of each event, and their subsequent interpretations, feelings and how they were impacted, I am certain, they would each be unique and in many cases, vary completely from my own. It would be futile and unnecessary to explore and explain everyone's side of the story related to each event. It is instead sufficient to say, that I own my interpretations and perceptions and see them as neither factual nor true.

My beliefs were generated as a sum total of my own ego and my own need to be right about what I imagined to be true, and it is this interpretation that matters the most as it is the one that has allowed me to realize the greatest transformation in the quality of all of these relationships.

Through letting go of the old interpretations and beliefs I learned how to cast off the label of being "Larry's brother," and it had nothing to do with Larry or anyone else. Instead, I learned to be my authentic self. I gave up living life as though I didn't matter, and I learned what it meant to *lead*, beginning with leading myself. I learned how to redesign my attitude, and in turn, I altered the choices I was making that impacted all of my relationships. Since that important time of discovery and growth, I've been living up to my vision and living up to the belief that I can create anything I want, anything I declare. My past no longer determines the future for me.

I'm certain there are a lot of people who have grown up in circumstances that were either equally or more challenging than my own. Others may have experienced a more pleasant childhood than I did. Either way, I don't see myself—or my past—as better or worse than anyone else's life story. I see myself as an example of what is possible for people when we learn how to use our minds, our hearts, and our wisdom, to create greater possibilities than the ones we previously thought were available to us. Many of us have experienced wasting our talents, our gifts, and our extraordinary potential by allowing damaging thoughts and beliefs to hold us down, to keep us stuck, and to eventually undermine or sabotage what we are fully capable of creating.

About one year later, in January of 1987, I started working for the Lifespring Corporation and developing myself as a trainer and coach—just as I'd imagined on that first night of my first training. I was basically the low man on the totem pole when I started out in a sales position. I said, "I don't care what I have to do or what it's going to take, but I want to become a master leader, a role model, a human being who people will respect, admire, and seek out."

I worked hard and developed myself rigorously. After three months, I got promoted to a higher-level position and continued gaining promotions within the company over several years. I achieved the highest levels of success rapidly and exceeded the expectations for all of my jobs and positions. I broke records in producing results and often held not only one position, but two at the same time. My salary increased every year, with raises which reflected the excellence of my performance.

By the time I was twenty-five years old, I was put in charge of my own business center in Fort Lauderdale, Florida. When I took over, the business center was ranked 11th out of twelve centers, second from the bottom. I was given six months to turn it around from red to black, or Lifespring was going to close the office. The president of the company, John Hanley, told me he didn't want to waste my talent and ability in a business center that had been unsuccessful and unprofitable since it opened about three years earlier. He gave me my shot to show what I could really do, and the difference I could truly make. It was 100% up to me—my responsibility and my opportunity.

I'll never forget my first day of work in Fort Lauderdale. We held a meeting and invited all the people who were working with the office to help build it and make it a success. I stood in front of everyone at twenty-five years old (and, barely even shaving at the time, looking like I was eighteen), and I declared my vision. I said, emphatically, "I declare our Florida center is the number one center in all of Lifespring, from this moment on." I said it not because there was any hard evidence or any logical reason to believe it would actually happen, but because *I said so*. I was standing on the Skinny Branches, declaring from the vision I had made up in my mind: I believed wholeheartedly that by working together with the staff and volunteers, we could accomplish great things. This declaration was made regardless of circumstances, history, three years of mediocre results, and a complete lack of belief in the possibility of success. Before, in my past, I had thought very little of myself, always making excuses and thinking, "I can't, it's not possible, I'm not worthy." I had been fighting to be right about those perceived limitations. But now I had transformed that belief into self-confidence. Now I thought to myself, "*Whatever I say, I can do.*" This was not coming from a place of ego or arrogance, or even a misguided need to prove myself. I was simply taking ownership of the power of my word and my vision to make it real. My focus was simply on what could be.

In my speech, I imagined the possibility of transforming the community in Florida from an environment where people go to retire and begin the final chapters of their lives, to a place where people live, thrive, and invent new possibilities to make a significant difference in the quality of their life. I dreamt of transforming Florida into a paradise of tropical beauty where people wanted to live, not die. We would begin with the people we love most, and then spread out to our friends, our co-workers, our neighbors down the street, people across the town and in the next city, until we could ultimately reach people around the world. We would create a shining example for others to follow. The others in the room were inspired like never before. I surrounded myself with like-minded leaders, maniacs on a mission. These were people who cared about other people, and cared so much about the vision and success of the company that it was as if they actually owned it themselves. Over time, I hired and trained dozens of leaders and partners to work together with me. Our relationship didn't exist only in a business setting—we treated each other as family. We loved each other. We went to each other's weddings and birthday celebrations. We celebrated childbirths together, and in some very sad cases, attended the funerals of each other's loved ones. We fought *for* each other, not *with* each other. We fought for the possibilities, for our students and for ourselves. My business center in Fort Lauderdale became the number one center in one short year. We went from red to black. We blew the roof off of all financial expectations.

I was honored by my superiors, my colleagues, my peers, my employees, and by the most important people of all, our students. By the time I was twenty-seven, I was promoted to National Training Director. The company would send all of the hot new employee prospects to work specifically with me and my amazing office staff. They were looking for us to train, coach, and develop them so that they would have the same level of success and effectiveness I was producing with my center. This was a great honor for me. I wasn't only achieving the success and receiving the accolades I wanted from my work, I was also starting to receive the recognition I'd always wanted from my family.

Around this time, I remember having a conversation with my dad, Bob. He told me that during a family conversation, he'd asked my mother, Larry, Danielle, and Candide one of his infamous questions. He'd said, "If we were all stranded on an island, and we had to choose who we thought should be the leader of our family, who would each of you pick?" I was shocked to find out that my family had voted for me. What? Me? I went from the dog-house to the penthouse? Could this really be possible? But wait a minute, what about Larry? He's the "perfect prince," isn't he?

When I say that transformation is possible, I mean that transformation is *really* possible. If I can create it and do what I have been able to do in my own life, then anyone can. I not only believe it as a result of my own experiences, but thousands of people I have coached over the last thirty years have enjoyed the same outcome.

How many people think they have to eat dinner before they're allowed to have dessert? Life is not only about struggling, work-ing, and overcoming burdens and obligations. You don't have to suffer through the best years of your life without ever allowing yourself to smell the roses along the way. You may think you're not allowed to experience joy, abundance, and easy living until you've paid your dues. But you would be wrong, because your quality of life is going downhill faster than a snowball going down a mountain. Before you know it, it's over. Game, set, and match.

During the nearly ten years I worked with Lifespring, I became the top trainer and coach in the company, and opportunities were opening up for me like never before. I envisioned creating a company of my own and stepping up and out onto the Skinny Branches once more. I was well aware that I would be taking a huge risk. After all, about 98% of all new companies fail and close within two years. Did I really want to give up an estab-lished career, a newfound credibility, and above all, a comfort-able life? But I had achieved all I imagined within the company and excelled at all levels. With my confidence high and my limit-ing past stories no longer in charge of my life, I saw myself as a budding entrepreneur.

So, in 1997, I left the security of Lifespring and started my own company. My new company, Direct Impact, was one of the very first companies in the world to offer Executive Coaching, Organi-zational Transformation, and Personal Coaching. In my first year of business, I was working with businesses on every level: Fortune 500 companies, mid-sized companies, and my favorite, other start-up companies by visionary entrepreneurs. I coached and helped these powerful, influential owners, CEOs, and company presidents to create extraordinary results in their professional and personal lives. During the past twenty years, I have coached and worked with dozens of organizations to create leadership, company visions, championship teams, profitability, new products and services, communication skills, conflict resolution, inspiration, motivation, sales training, and strategic planning. I have helped in hiring and identifying future stars, mastering public speaking skills, providing powerful feedback, and acting as a sounding board.

In 2004, I started another company with my partner, fellow trainer, and good friend Chris Lee. It's called Impacto Vital, and we serve the country of Puerto Rico. Impacto Vital is the number one transformational training company on the island and has been for over ten years now. We have had over 10,000 students take our leadership development classes. From our business center in Puerto Rico, we opened offices in Santo Domingo, Dominican Republic; Mexico City, Mexico; Guadalajara, Mexico; Miami, Florida; Denver, Colorado; and New York, New York. We have trained and developed dozens of trainers and coaches to become experts in our coaching technology and they are now working and serving communities and countries all over the world. Working with Chris is, and has been, one of the great joys and accomplishments in my life. I went from being his coach, to being his mentor, to being his friend. And now he is my business partner and my peer. How amazing is that feeling we get when we hold people to their highest possibilities, and they shine like stars?

Living on the Skinny Branches changed my life. Now I live a life of vision and courage. I take risks in my relationships and in my career. I do what is uncomfortable, which leads to better physical heath, financial abundance, and contribution to others. I don't sit back and revel in past successes. I live in the present.

I'm always asking myself: *Who can I be today? What can I do today? What am I committed to generating today?* When I'm on the Skinny Branches, I know that I am alive because I'm experiencing life at its fullest. Most people merely exist; they're not truly *alive*. Most people are merely surviving, not expanding. Most people are breathing, eating, and sleeping, all of which are necessary for survival but not sufficient for actual *living*.

When you're on the Skinny Branches of the tree of life, you *are* alive. You can feel every cell in your body. You can feel your heart beating, the hair on your skin. You experience the air that expands your lungs and sense the nourishment of oxygen. In such moments, you can imagine and see every possibility. You can see the forest *and* the trees, and you can appreciate both. You can see an infinite and limitless future from your spot on the Skinny Branches. You can get closer to the stars and be completely connected to your own cells at the same time. You can start living in unprecedented ways because you have removed the limitations, both real and perceived, that before seemed like impossible barriers.

When you're on the Skinny Branches of the tree of life, you're inventing; you're creating; you're passionate about your vision *and* completely vulnerable to it. Your heart is open. You're going after what matters to you with urgency, and you realize your life is *now*. You're not just thinking about what you want, by procrastinating and pondering the possibility. You're in committed action mode, and you're *at risk*. The Skinny Branches are 100% about being in a consistent and rigorous state of risk.

Living on the Skinny Branches is about having the genuine belief that everyone has dreams, and that everyone has the capability to make those dreams real. Unfortunately, dreaming occurs mostly while we're asleep. The sad fact is that many of us are still sleeping during the day. Metaphorically, we're asleep at the wheel and using automatic pilot to get by. Autopilot isn't necessarily a bad thing. It's okay. But how many people have been conditioned to believe that mediocrity is a sufficient way to live? The typical response to the question, "How are you?" has now become, "I'm fine, I'm okay, thanks." If people truly knew what was possible for them in their lives, there is no way they would be okay with being okay. If they were conscious about the choices they were making and the ways they were limiting themselves, it would not be fine. Automatic pilot is unfulfilling and unsatisfying for a human being with dreams and future possibilities.

No one wants to be in a marriage that's just *fine*. No one wants their children to be *okay*. To describe your experience of life and living as *okay* is, quite frankly, anything but okay. The opportunity of living on the Skinny Branches is to embody the very essence of living life at the highest level possible. It is to excel at living.

Think of yourself as the star of a movie. That movie is called YOUR LIFE. You are no longer an extra, barely making the final cut. You are a champion, and champions always play to win. You may not be able to play the game of basketball like NBA super-star LeBron James. But you can operate from a similar context of vision, excellence, dedication, and determination. He knew when he was ten years old that someday, he would be the best bas-ketball player in the world, and a world champion. How has he done so far?

As Mark Twain once stated, "Let us endeavor to live so that when we come to die, even the undertaker will be sorry."

NOW IT'S YOUR TURN TO LIVE.

Chapter Two

EMPOWERING YOURSELF

CREATING A LIFE WORTH LIVING begins with recognizing and facing yourself honestly. You need to be willing to tell the truth, the whole truth, and nothing but the truth. During this recognition process, you must allow yourself to experience and confront the underlying beliefs, conversations, interpretations, and thoughts that cause you to make the decisions and choices you make. In order to empower yourself, you first need to address what's stopping you. In other words, what's actually in the way of your empowerment?

Consider this: When we're born, we come into the world as a blank canvas, a clean slate with no set beliefs or interpretations. We are completely vulnerable and open. We see the world through our openness; we are sponges soaking in the world around us. We use all of our senses, fully experiencing every sight, sound, smell, taste, and touch. The German philosopher Immanuel Kant believed that our ability to understand the world around us begins with our own view through an individual lens. Our senses are undeveloped when we are born and as we grow physically, in height and weight, we also grow mentally, in the way our brain functions and in our ability to discern the constant information we are receiving.

Initially, we have no judgments, no limitations, no assessments, no opinions, and no point of view. We are simply human beings who don't do anything but absorb. We have no filters and no ability to process the information we are receiving. Early on, we learn how to get food, how to make noise, and how to communicate, even though we don't yet have the words or the ability to formulate sentences. We learn our names, who our parents and siblings are, and of course, what is ours. And what *is* ours? For a newborn baby, absolutely everything.

In our early years, we develop an understanding of words and of language itself. Learning to speak obviously helps us to communicate our wants, needs, and fears. It is an essential tool for sharing this amazing curiosity we're experiencing. How important is our ability to communicate? The theoretical physicist Stephen Hawking once said, "For millions of years, mankind lived like animals. Then something happened which unleashed the power of our imagination. We learned to talk and we learned to listen. Speech has allowed the communication of ideas, enabling human beings to work together to build the impossible." When we were young children, life was full of non-stop surprises, and new discoveries happened every day. We were fascinated with life and the world we came to live in. Similar to how Columbus discovered the New World, we were discovering *our* new world.

As we're in the process of becoming human beings, our bodies are growing, and our ability to interpret and decipher information is developing. During this time, we begin construction on what psychologists refer to as a "comfort zone." Through their research, they've come to the overwhelming conclusion that by the time we are approximately seven years old, the main structure of our comfort zone will have been designed. They believe that by that age, we will have already invented this self-actualized and self-limiting box. Essentially, we will spend the remainder of our lives reinforcing the beliefs and interpretations that keep us in the box. Look at your life right now. What are your beliefs about yourself? What limiting beliefs do you have that keep you inside your unique comfort zone? Where do those beliefs come from? How does your comfort zone distort your view of the world that exists outside of you? Given what's possible in our lives, why do we choose to be in a box of any kind, for any reason?

Once we create our comfort zones and the beliefs that keep us inside them, each and every experience, decision, and moment, is now filtered through the comfort zone and those same beliefs. Imagine a spaghetti strainer and visualize the water seeping through the holes. Now imagine life and all of its wonders being filtered through this same process. Information is no longer neutral—it's distorted through your beliefs. The famous physicist Heisenberg created the Uncertainty Principle, which roughly states that it's impossible to maintain objectivity because we are influenced by our own beliefs. The truth is not really *the* truth—it's *a* truth or *your* truth. There are facts, and then there are interpretations. They are not the same thing. Interpretations and beliefs are created as a reaction, a defense mechanism, to our experiences and the significant events in our lives. We tell ourselves that the space inside the box is safe, while everything outside the box is scary or dangerous. Maybe you remember the robot from the 1970s T.V. classic and cult hit *Lost In Space*, repeating the same phrase in every episode: "Warning, Will Robinson, danger, danger!" This is the inner voice of your comfort zone.

Another way to see it is, by the time we are seven years old we are already operating from our comfort zone. Another word you can use for comfort zone is EGO. They can essentially be used to mean the same thing. We all have ego and people will often misinterpret the meaning of the word. They'll say, "So-and-so has a big ego." Yes, one form of ego is arrogance: a feeling of superiority, the notion that you are always right, that you are better and smarter than other people. But the definition of ego in the realm of psychology is much more ordinary and basic, and it is a disease we all share. Ego is the separate, isolated self. It's seeing the world as separate from you. It's also seeing yourself as separate from the world around you, as different from other people: *I am me, you are you, and we are not the same.* We are individuals. In the beginning of those first stages when we develop this mindset of being separate from other people and the world around us, ego isn't a negative thing. We don't see it as a limitation because we're too young to understand our thoughts and comprehend their meanings or effects. We're only small children. How could we know?

Over time, as we get older, the comfort zone, our ego, begins to actually feel like an imaginary wall around us. The walls become reinforced primarily and specifically with events that cause us to experience pain or hurt feelings. I refer to these events as "buttons." A button is an event in our lives that automatically triggers a certain degree of emotional reaction. This emotion could be pain, sadness, anger, frustration, guilt, shame, resentment, blame, sorrow, or insecurity, and it often leads to a strong desire to shut down, disconnect, and avoid. We learn to avoid in a lot of ways. For example, we can avoid pain and hurt by working, sleeping, watching TV, eating, surfing the internet, cleaning, drinking, talking on the phone, dealing with someone else's issues, gossiping, doing busy work, having sex, doing drugs, etc. What are some of the ways you attempt to avoid in your daily life? What exactly are you avoiding?

Some other buttons could include your position growing up as the oldest child, the middle child, or the "baby" of the family. It could be witnessing your parents arguing or fighting, or being criticized and ripped apart for every little thing. Maybe you were laughed at in school. Maybe your parents divorced, you didn't make the team, your teachers gave you a hard time in school, or you were bullied. Or maybe you didn't get enough attention as a child because you had a large family and time was limited. Maybe your family moved around a lot. Maybe people judged you because you weren't the same as everyone else: different skin color, religion, culture, accent, clothes. Maybe you were simply different from the "norm." All of these experiences contribute to the creation of your limiting beliefs. Take a moment to think about what your most dominant limiting beliefs are. When was the first time you remember thinking or feeling that way? What was the specific event or experience that triggered it? Who was involved? How did it make you feel? What did you decide about yourself? About the people involved? Write down your answers to these questions. Take as much time as you need. Take note of any strong emotions along the way. You have complete permission to experience your emotions, whatever they may be. Not only is it okay to feel them, it's essential in the process of creating a genuine transformation. When you're ready, continue reading on.

For some of you, there are events that were even more significant than what we've just discussed. These would be considered traumatic events. A "red flag" event. These types of events, especially the ones that occurred in our early childhood, are the ones that have the greatest impact on our comfort zone and our limiting beliefs. Without a powerful coaching session, a therapist intervention, or a transformational training experience, these limiting beliefs can often become permanent.

Examples of "red flag" traumas could be the death of a family member; physical, mental, verbal, emotional, and/or sexual abuse; or alcoholism and drug addiction with the majority of these offenses committed by your mom, your dad, or both. As painful, uncomfortable, or embarrassing as it may be, think about whether there were any traumatic events that occurred in your formative years. How old were you when they happened? Who was involved? What did you decide about yourself when it happened? What did you decide about others as a result of these traumas? What are the beliefs you then created about men, women, people in general, and the world at large?

I want you to draw a box on a blank piece of paper and put a symbol in the center. That symbol represents you, the authentic you. This is the version of you that was born into the world with infinite possibilities. Now, write all of your limiting beliefs inside the box, and think about how those beliefs are stopping you from experiencing what you want in your life. Maybe you're thinking, "I'm not good enough. I'm not smart enough. I'm stupid. Something's wrong with me. I don't fit in. I don't belong. I don't trust. I can't. I'm alone." Or maybe you have an even more aggressive and destructive interpretation: "I hate myself. I'm not lovable. I'm worthless. I'm dirty. My life doesn't matter. My mother is horrible and mean. My father is heartless and has no feelings. My mother is selfish. My father doesn't care about us at all. I'll never be successful."

Over time, these interpretations fail to stay flexible. They become permanent and fixed as if they are hard facts for us. *We* take the experiences we have as a result of the events and turn them into these self-righteous interpretations. Through this process, we form not only our ego but also our "ego conversations," and now everything that happens in our life is filtered through these beliefs that we've created.

Once we formulate our ego, we reinforce it with every passing year. Life goes faster and faster. Look back to your teenage years and remember how you reinforced the beliefs you had already created. For example, at sixteen years old, there was a girl you were attracted to, and you wanted to ask her out on a date.

Remember the agony you put yourself through? "What if she says no? I'll be destroyed. What if she rejects me?" All of your fears were going crazy inside. Where do the fears come from? They come from your past experiences and your interpretations of the events in your life. At times, you probably had so many voices in your head, you might have thought you were going crazy, just like I did. All the voices: "She's not gonna like me. I'm not good enough. I'm not smart enough. I'm not handsome enough. I'm not lovable. She would like me if I were more like Larry." Maybe you wanted to be a doctor, but no one in your family had even gone to college. Here come the voices: "I'm not worthy. I can't. It's not possible. We can't afford it. I guess I'll settle on being a nurse; it's more practical, logical. I'm a woman and the path is harder for me."

Maybe you dreamed of being a professional athlete, an astronaut, a pilot, a business owner, or a rich, successful entrepreneur. It doesn't matter what you dream of, by the time you develop your comfort zone and ego, your future has already been determined for you by guess who? YOU! You can point your finger at mom and dad, your brother, men or women in general, the whole world, but none of that will ever make a difference. It won't change the situation you're in. All your finger-pointing will do is make you "right." What matters to you more, being right or having the life you want?

The first step to creating a life worth living is to realize that everything we see, think, feel, touch, taste, and hear, is subject to interpretation. Everything is a conversation, not a fact. Hundreds and hundreds of years ago, the Europeans thought the earth was flat. That belief limited the way they lived and the choices they had at their disposal. Reality is a figment of our imaginations. We invent our own reality. The honor and privilege of being a human being is the power to transform our own reality and create new choices in our lives.

I've lived long enough to see the first man land on the moon, to see the space shuttle program launched, and now it's been retired.

Who would have ever believed in the last thirty years that NASA would struggle to obtain the funding necessary to continue operating? The power of our ability to convince ourselves and others of nearly anything is both exciting and scary at the same time. The power of interpretation is much like a double-edged sword.

Let's begin anew. Let's use our inner voices to our advantage, to work *for* us instead of *against* us. Let's align our private thoughts with our public communications. Some people are meek and feel self-conscious about affirming who they are and what they want. The thing about fear is that it's just fear. The fear of ridicule, the fear of failure, even the fear of success—they seem real, but they're imagined. We need to build strength within in order to gain the power to overcome those fears. This strength will allow you to stand up to the criticism and judgment of the naysayers and the perceived naysayers.

You can never move up and go out on the Skinny Branches if you're afraid of what others will say. You can never achieve the life that makes *you* happy by conforming to the opinions of the masses. You must take ownership of your own desires and fuel your dreams. The first step is giving yourself the power, the will, and the permission to desire a life worth living. Only then can you vow to do what it takes to actually achieve that life. Your inner voice will usually start off with a judgment, a criticism, or a fear, which then prohibits you from creating what you want. We need to interrupt the autopilot of that little voice. We need to realize that we are in charge of the incoming and outgoing messages of our minds. As humans, we can be mentally lazy. All too often, we allow ourselves to be swallowed up by the constant disempowerment of this inner dialogue. We reinforce it and enable it by allowing it to exist in the first place. The philosopher Martin Heidegger once said, "Man acts as though he were the shaper and master of language, while in fact, language remains the shaper of man."

Let's create what I call an internal mantra—a commitment you make to yourself and to the world around you. This mantra is much more than a simple sound, noise, or affirmation. It's a declaration of the essence of who you are. This mantra is an internal agreement or a contract that you're making with yourself. Not only that, this mantra is the act of declaring who you are from your genuine, authentic self.

What if you weren't all the negative thoughts you had made up about yourself, who would you be? Who are you underneath all the masks, rackets, and facades. I want you to choose three adjectives that describe who you truly are. Three adjectives that resonate from within. When you say them, they should sound and feel like a ping, not a thud. When you have these adjectives in mind, start to interrupt those limiting conversations with yourself. Start to interrupt the little voice inside yourself by repeating your mantra over and over again, by saying, "I am a..."

I empower you to do it, to take a risk. On the count of three, I want you to say it out loud. Begin with the words, "I am a...," and follow it with the words that you've decided describe your authentic self. Imagine you are having a celebration of life party on the Skinny branches of the tree and the only way that people will come is if they can hear you. On the count of three, I want you to say it out loud.

One, two, three: "I am a..."

Every time you hear the internal little voice saying, "Oh no, you can't do it," interrupt that conversation by repeating your inner mantra. Let's say that you've decided your mantra will go like this: "I am a powerful, loving, worthy leader." Saying that statement out loud automatically interrupts all the other rackets, judgments, and limiting beliefs that are bouncing around inside your head. It interrupts the internal conversation because it's a powerful statement that reveals who you are, your authentic being. If you say it over and over again, it becomes a mantra. A mantra can create the energy and confidence needed to allow you to take action, to get out there in the world and create the results you have always wanted. Turn the volume down on your ego, and turn the volume up on your mantra. It deserves to be heard.

When you are choosing your adjectives, think not only about what you want in life, but also about whom you want to be, and what you want other people to say about you. People will always talk about us, whether we like it or not. They will always have opinions, judgments, criticisms, put-downs, denigrations, etc. Can we stop this negative behavior or change it completely? The honest answer is both yes and no. By taking charge of our inner dialogue, we can generate the ways of being we're committed to with many people around us, primarily in our most connected relationships. Why? Because they will be the most receptive to our changes and want the best for us.

It might take us more time to win over other people, such as co-workers, bosses, partners, strangers, estranged family members, and even former lovers, but it is absolutely possible. Think of the famous quote from the movie *Field of Dreams*: "If you build it, they will come." If you'll remember, the film's protagonist, Ray, played by Kevin Costner, builds a baseball field in the middle of his farmland in Iowa. He doesn't know why he's doing it, only that he keeps hearing voices he can't ignore. By listening to and following the requests of the voices, he eventually comes to realize they are messages from his dad, who passed away years earlier. They are messages from a father who wants to see his son and actually connect with him for the first time, the father Ray never knew. As long as we have breath, we have the power to make the impossible, possible.

When creating your mantra, be sure to choose adjectives that will demand and bring out the highest version of yourself. When I'm coaching people, I usually ask them to focus on adjectives that are in direct conflict with their comfort zones. For example, let's say somebody has trust issues. How can she take this into account when creating her mantra? She could start by saying, "I am a trusting, vulnerable, and risk-taking person." That statement immediately interrupts her inherent lack of trust. Let's say somebody else is fearful. Instead of his mantra being, "I am a scared, small, and insignificant person," it would be, "I am a worthy, brave, and powerful person." Choosing to be brave can minimize and possibly dissolve your fear. Because bravery is the opposite of fear. Likewise, if somebody is insecure: "I am a confident person." If somebody else is afraid to open his or her heart, afraid to show emotion: "I am loving. I am intimate." It's a simple way of interrupting the little voice inside your head, interrupting your comfort zone, interrupting limiting conversations and rackets, and interrupting those behaviors that are not consistent with your vision of a life worth living.

When you are afraid to do or say something in your daily life, you can say your mantra over and over again until it drowns out and interrupts that particular fear. Once you succeed in doing that, you can finally step out powerfully into the game of life. You can take those risky steps you've been avoiding in your work. You can make those cold calls because you don't care what people think of you and you're no longer afraid of rejection. You can go into that staff meeting and empower your executive team to set new goals and missions for your companies. You can now possess the confidence to have the conversation with your husband about having your first child, which you've been avoiding. You can ask your boss for the raise you feel you have earned. You can find the energy to achieve the level of health you want through self-discipline, willpower, and determination to exercise and change your dietary habits. You can open your heart to the person you have feelings for. In short, you can do everything you've always been too afraid to do. Your mantra gives you the power and the confidence to go after your vision, to create a life worth living. When you're willing to say it out loud, it becomes a public declaration. It's one thing to think privately to yourself: *I am a worthy, powerful, confident leader*, or *I am a passionate, courageous, joyful leader.* It's another thing to say it out loud. Your willingness to say it out loud is a reflection of your commitment, courage, and leadership. That's what it takes to be an inspiration to the rest of the world around you. When you say your mantra out loud, you are VULNERABLE. You show up shamelessly authentic, without caring whether it makes you look good, without caring what other people will think, and without fear of rejection. By doing this, you give everyone else something to aspire to be. You hold the power to inspire them, too.

Think of your mantra as an interpersonal declaration of independence from the past. Our past is our comfort zone. Our past is our ego. Our past is our limiting belief. Our past represents our habits, the way we've always done things. This statement serves as an interruption to that behavior. In essence, you are declaring yourself free from your past. You are lifting up your anchor and setting sail for unchartered waters, the open sea. You're saying, "From this moment on, I'm a passionate, loving, giving woman. I'm an outrageous, risk-taking, honest man. I'm a vulnerable, beautiful, confident leader. I am a sexy, authentic, committed leader." You declare three personalized adjectives that are consistent with *your* vision, consistent with *your* values, consistent with what it will take for *you* to get from A to Z, from where you are now to where you want to be. You declare it, and it becomes an interruption to your status quo, just as the Declaration of Independence was for the United States in 1776.

This mantra holds that same kind of power, albeit on a smaller scale. In spite of any lack of evidence, lack of reason, or lack of logic, you are using your mantra to declare who you are from this point forward. By arresting and interrupting your autopilot, by retraining your mind to be the source of possibility, of your life, your future, and your vision, by retraining yourself to be the author of your life, by declaring who you are—you have the power you need to actually do it.

If you are consistent with this way of living every day, you will eventually create momentum, confidence, and a new belief in who you are and who you can be. Your focus is on creating the future, not dwelling on the past. Living on the Skinny Branches means living your life with courage, passion, and freedom. When I talk about life on the Skinny Branches, I'm talking about leaving behind a life of mediocrity and survival. Instead, we move into abundant thinking. We move to creating, to declaring. Life on the Skinny Branches is about declaring what we want, and having the nerve to do it publicly with specificity. When a person tells a single friend privately that she wants to lose some weight, it's not a "real" declaration. It's only a vision with no commitment—it's a fantasy, a nice idea, and there is nothing at stake.

Being on the Skinny Branches of the tree requires a declaration that propels and even forces you to commit. It puts you in a position to do something that you've never done before, something that is important to you. You commit to creating something without any evidence that you'll be successful. This commitment is not based on the past, nor is it a reaction to the past. Instead, it's based on something that you're intrinsically empowered to create. You want to achieve something that's important to you, something that will transform your whole way of being.

In order to reclaim power from our ego and the victim stories from our pasts, it's important to clarify the distinct definition of responsibility. Often when people say, "I am responsible," what they actually mean is, "I did something wrong. I messed up. Something horrible has already occurred, and I am to blame for it. I am at fault. I am guilty." Their version of responsibility occurs after the breakdown, after the fact. In many instances, people say they're responsible so the other person will reply, "I forgive you," and let it go. We often say we are responsible in an attempt to pacify our problems or issues, but we don't actually resolve them.

A powerful definition of responsibility is to be the sole, uncontested author of your life. It means to stand as the source of everything, including the past, present, and future. This interpretation of responsibility does not come from a place of ego or arrogance, but from a place of ownership. John F. Kennedy famously said, "Victory has a thousand fathers, but defeat is an orphan." It's easy to declare responsibility when things are going your way, isn't it? When she says "yes" to your marriage proposal, or "I do" at the wedding. When you close that business deal. When the traffic disappears and you make your flight. When you get the raise. When people compliment you on how young you look. Taking credit for success or good fortune and being truly responsible are not the same thing. Responsibility actually begins during the conceptualization of an idea. Responsibility begins in the original thought. Responsibility is present when you first make a choice; it doesn't appear suddenly after you've seen the results of that choice. Responsibility happens in the concept; it happens in the origination.

A key aspect of creating a life worth living is adopting a set of values that you can use to filter the choices and commitments that you make. Let's say you make a public declaration to lose weight, instead of only making an idle comment during a casual chat with a friend over a latte. It's out in the open now. You declare: "I'm committed to losing twenty pounds in the next forty-five days. To do so, I'm going to work out a minimum of five days a week, doing forty-five minutes of cardio. I'm also committed to designing a diet that is consistent with my goal of losing those twenty pounds. I'm not doing it because my mother thinks I'm fat. I'm not doing it because other people are talking about my weight behind my back. I'm not even doing it because I don't like the way I look. I'm doing it because I said so. I am responsible, I matter, and I want to live the healthiest life possible." Now that's a whole different way of looking at it. It's a whole different way to focus on it. Life on the Skinny Branches is about living. Imagine having so much confidence in your declaration to lose weight that you actually go out and buy yourself a new outfit in the size you've decided you'll be in the future. Now that is a person operating at the highest level of responsibility.

What does it mean to live fully? Living fully means that if you feel love, you express it. You shout it from the rooftops. You don't withhold it, hide it, or disguise it. You express it with unbridled passion. You don't want life to be a constant refrain of *shoulda, woulda, coulda*. You live your life knowing that life itself is precious, that life is important, that the people in your life shouldn't just "know" you care. They shouldn't just have a vague concept of your love. They should get to experience your love in an unapologetic, vulnerable, and shameless way.

Creating on the Skinny Branches of the tree is about creating profound love with your children and your spouse. I take action every day to show my wife that I not only love her, but that I'm *in* love with her. I don't just buy her flowers or gifts, which anyone with money can easily do. I don't just say the words "I love you" every other day. I find ways to communicate my love to her, to let her know how special she is to me. I take committed action daily to create the experience of love for her and with her. I can do this in a variety of simple but effective ways: by listening to her talk about her work day, by discussing the children and our family schedules, by offering my support in managing our plans, by going grocery shopping, by doing the laundry and the dishes, by taking out the garbage (without her having to ask—a key distinction), by watching a show together and using TiVo to save my ball games for later (when she's sleeping), by taking her to a movie I know she'll want to see, or by taking her shopping. She does so much for our family that thinking about herself is usually her last priority. So I'll say to her, "Babe, you think about everyone else, I'm here to think about you."

There are infinite ways for you to create the experience of profound love with your lover, girlfriend, life partner, or future partner. The distinction of love requires your full participation and contribution. Caring enough to know what's important to your partner is the key to a successful and lasting connection. Take the time to find thoughtful gifts, instead of simply buying an expensive but meaningless piece of jewelry. Show up to events, support her, make her feel that you care. The priceless moments are the experiences she will remember. Time spent coexisting in the same room, staring ahead at the TV, or reading the news on your iPad, is not QUALITY TIME. It's a slow and painful death to a love that once flourished, to a respect and admiration that was once invincible, to a partnership that once was on the cutting edge and a model for all.

Here's another example: I know my wife loves music. It's an interest we share and something we both care about. However, she likes pop music while I prefer rock and roll. But I still turn to iTunes and spend substantial time searching for a special song, a love song that will touch my wife and let her know how much I love her, how much I care. I will make sure it's a song *she* will love, even if our music tastes are not the same. My iPod is full of music from Pink, Adele, Colbie Caillat, Katy Perry, and of course, Maroon 5. Now that's real love for an old rock and roller like me.

Living on the Skinny Branches of the tree could be about love in a romantic relationship. It could also be about communicating with your children, creating a bond and an everlasting connection with them. I have very deep, intimate, and personal relationships with both of my kids, Nicholas and Savannah, even when I'm not physically with them. I live in Dallas. They live in Phoenix. But I know where they are each and every day. I know where they are because their day-to-day joy and happiness matter to me and I care. I have a strong relationship with them. I hear what they say. I listen to their words, their thoughts, their concerns. I learn what's important to them, where they want to go, and what they want to do in their lives. Anyone can have a child, and a lot of people put in the work of raising children, but not all parents are in a real, communicating relationship with their children. Not all parents are truly part of their children's lives, especially after the kids are grown and on their own. Being a parent is an honor and a privilege. It's a blessing, not a job or an obligation.

We don't live in a vacuum. Therefore, creating a life worth living isn't only about you. It's also about how you interact with life's daily surprises. Do you look at challenging situations as obstacles, or do you see them as opportunities? Do you look at them as problems that need to be solved or as gifts you receive with open arms? Do you look at life from all possible angles, or do you stubbornly insist that your way is always right? Creating a life worth living is not about survival. It's not about existing. It's not about settling for mediocrity. It's about stepping into the concept of living, stepping into the practice of living, in all aspects of your life. This includes your professional life, your health, your relationships with people, and even your relationships with money.

In today's society, people often have a dysfunctional relationship with money. It shows up in both major and minor ways. People are in debt. People mortgage their future with the "I'll pay later" mentality. People are in scarcity. People attach their self-worth to their bank account. How they feel about themselves depends on how much money they're making and how much they have saved. Their self-worth equals their actual monetary worth in life. That's the sign of a dysfunctional relationship.

I frequently see incredibly talented people settling for mediocre jobs that don't suit them instead of creating new possibilities, living up to their potential, and thriving in their life. Creating a life worth living is about looking at your job, looking at your career, looking at how much money you make, then asking yourself, "Is this what I want? Is this what I'm worth? Is this what I'm capable of?" If the answer to these questions is no, then how has your relationship with money affected your results? It's time to get off the treadmill to examine what it is you truly want. Think about a career that would be a great fit for you—a job that would support you financially but still challenge you intellectually. Find work that will be fulfilling for you at the end of the day. Are you an entrepreneur at heart? Consider starting your own business. Have you been waiting for the "right" time? Ask yourself this:

How long have I been waiting, and what is the price I'm paying for not pursuing my business dreams? Think of your career and work as a vehicle to support you in achieving the lifestyle you want, not as a prison sentence with limited visitation rights, making license plates for less than minimum wage because this is what you believe you are worth.

We have the ability to stand in the middle of a challenge and see the Skinny Branches, see the forest for the trees, see the possibilities, the stars. How often were we told as children that the sky is the limit? Yet, years later, we're living a mediocre life. We're waiting to win the jackpot in the lottery. We're waiting for a miracle to happen, for a bluebird to land in our lap. We're waiting for society to change. We're waiting for the "right person" to magically appear. We're waiting for Congress to pass legislation. We're waiting for the economy to get better. We're waiting for the President to lead. But there are many examples of people who were able—in spite of the odds, the rough circumstances, and the challenges—to rise above. Everyone can learn from the lessons these individuals teach us.

This book is about learning how to *rise above* and make a difference. Let's take a look at Martin Luther King, Jr. What did Dr. King possess that the other African American men and women didn't have? At the time, he was a preacher and was already committed to making a difference with his congregation and in the community. Ultimately, he was recognized as the father of the Civil Rights Movement in America. Though he was born and raised in Georgia, his educational pursuits brought him to Boston where he met his future wife, Coretta. Then in 1955, a couple of representatives from a church in Montgomery, Alabama came to meet with him to discuss the busing crisis. They said something to the effect of, "Mr. King, we've heard a lot about you. We know you're educated and well spoken, and we'd like you to come down to support us in what we're doing." At first he said no. Why would he put his family at risk? Why would he put his own life at risk? He was busy. He was serving the people in his congregation. He was making a difference right where he was. He could easily have argued, "I'm already doing my part. I don't need to do something bigger than what I'm doing right now."

But they came back again. They had another conversation with him, and this time, he agreed to go. He took the risk. Talk about living on the Skinny Branches of the tree! He took it one step further. He went into the eye of the hurricane, the center of the war on racism and segregation. He traveled to a region that was, at the time, one of the most overtly dangerous places in the U.S. for an African-American individual or family to live. He went anyway and had the courage to speak up, to declare his vision publicly. He reached for the microphone and talked and talked and kept talking about the voting rights of all Americans. He talked civil rights and equal rights. He talked about fairness and justice, things that were not at all popular in the South at that time. But he was willing to take the risk. He lived on the Skinny Branches of the tree.

Did Dr. King possess something that the average person didn't at least have the potential to obtain? Absolutely not. He is someone who had a vision. He saw the big picture. He saw what life could be like for everyone. And he took it upon himself to do the responsible thing. He saw himself as the source, and it was his responsibility to use his power to make the difference. He didn't stand on the sidelines watching. In one of the greatest quotes ever spoken by Martin Luther King, Jr., he stated, "The ultimate measure of a man is not where he stands in moments of comfort and convenience, but where he stands at times of challenge and controversy." What a powerful statement of responsibility and courage. What if you had the power to make a similar declaration within your family life? To heal the wounds of the past? I did, and in doing so, I made the impossible, possible.

Martin Luther King, Jr. could have been one of those people watching from the sidelines, saying the world could and should be different, but taking no action to do anything about it. He could have had the belief that it was someone else's responsibility.

Many people believed that nothing would ever change, that racism would always exist in the South, and that African Americans would never have equal rights. Can you imagine having no right to vote? Not only in the literal sense, but figuratively as well. And yet, Dr. King took it upon himself to take the action. He took the risk. He lived on the Skinny Branches of the tree. He went after his vision and his dream. He went after it with passion, and yes, he put his life at stake. He put his family's life at stake. For him, it was a worthwhile risk. For his wife, it was a worthwhile risk. And as a result, he ultimately made an extraordinary impact for his people. The law changed. The South changed. The whole country changed. Did his achievements eliminate racism from existing around the country? No, but it certainly was a significant step in the process of unifying our country and creating "one nation, under God" for everyone, including African Americans.

Nelson Mandela is another excellent example of someone who rose above. He was locked in an eight-foot prison cell for twenty-seven years. He came out of prison with a smile on his face. What look would you have on your face after being incarcerated unjustly for twenty-seven years? Imagine the toll it would take on you mentally, emotionally, physically, and spiritually, to live without the choices and freedoms we enjoy here in the United States. To be unable to live with your wife, to be unable to see and parent your children. To know you might never see your mother or father again. To only be allowed one visit per year. Imagine what it would be like to live without equal rights, civil rights, or the decency of human dignity.

Mandela had no direct communication with his wife or children while he was in prison, except through letters that could be sent and received once a year. Even though his freedom was taken from him without his choosing, his vision was always present. His unwavering faith in the world's possibilities allowed him to live on the Skinny Branches even from his prison cell. He was able to see that possibility, see his purpose, and live his purpose.

The South African government could do anything they wanted to his physical body. They could do anything they wanted to restrict his choices in life. They could throw everything at him, including abusing, neglecting, and beating him down, but they could not stop this man from visualizing and communicating his vision for his people in his country, both blacks and whites, living together in equality and unity.

Nelson Mandela became an *inspiration*. Many people who obtain power, who get elected for office or selected for high ranking positions in organizations, soon forget the values that got them the position in the first place. Not Mandela. When he became a free man, he was humbled to see his vision and dream realized. He became the President of South Africa. When he ran for President, he promised to have a government that represented all of his country's people, both white and black. He kept his promise and created legislation that benefited the entirety of his people, regardless of color, religion, tribe, financial status, or educational background.

Creating a life worth living often means putting yourself at the risk of rejection, public humiliation, judgment, and criticism. But sometimes you actually have to put your life itself at risk. Why? Because when something matters to you so deeply that it comes from the core of your innermost being—the very essence of who you are—it feels like the *only* choice. You must give power to your voice, take committed action, and be willing to put yourself on the line. The philosopher Max Weber once said, "The ethic of conviction and the ethic of responsibility are not opposites. They are complementary to one another." Could there be a better example of leadership and ethics than that of Mandela?

Martin Luther King, Jr. didn't say, "Hey, I have a dream," and whisper it to a friend at the coffee shop. He didn't ask this hypothetical friend to keep it a secret: "Keep it down; I don't want anyone to hear." He didn't sit alone in his house thinking about his dream, only to never share it. No, he stood in front of the masses in public and declared with conviction, "I have a dream." It wasn't a dream for just African American people, and it wasn't a dream against white people. It was a dream for all people: whites, African Americans, Jews, Protestants, Catholics, all people, all walks of life.

That vision, that dream, that purpose comes out of the idea of creating a life worth living. He was asking us to visualize a life, a community, a nation no longer functioning in survival mode, no longer simply existing, no longer standing on the sidelines watching and observing the continuation of a flawed culture. He asked people to take action and stand up with him in supporting this vision of what he saw was possible. To stand responsible for owning the issues and breakdowns which existed, and then to use the consciousness of responsibility to make a difference and make their vote count. He was one of many extraordinary historical figures who lived before us and now offer us a chance to look at their contributions, their innovations, the gifts they gave, and the infinite lessons we can learn from them.

If you could use that same power of declaration and responsibility, what would you do? Who could you become if you owned this power? Who decides if you have the power or not? Who is the captain of your ship? Personally, I use the lessons of these leaders to give me the inspiration to be a better father, a better husband, a better man, and most importantly, a better human being. The most valuable contributions of others are the ones that directly impact the quality of life, not just for a few, but for all.

I recently received a touching message from one of the employees in my company from Puerto Rico. He said, "Hey boss, I just want to let you know that everybody who works for you here in our office really loves you and cares about you." Who sends a note to their boss just to say, "I love you and I care about you"? To me, that's incredible feedback. That's a sign that I'm succeeding in creating a life worth living, not just leading a successful organization.

One of my personal lifetime visions was to become an entrepreneur. Larry and I have always had great ideas—in theory and in our own minds, of course. But there is a big difference between thinking about something you want to do and actually doing it. I wanted to create a transformational training and coaching company that would give me the freedom to use my skills, talents, and abilities to make a powerful difference in people's lives. To not only facilitate, but to feed my desire to author something and uniquely design my own workshops. I not only made it happen, but I'm continuously making it happen. Part of my vision was to surround myself with like-minded visionaries and entrepreneurs. Knowing that the people I work with love the job and care about what we do and the service that we provide is what matters most. But to know they also love and care about me, not only as a boss, but as a person as well? That means everything. While awake, we spend a majority of our daily lives in or at work, not with our families or loved ones. So imagine surrounding yourself with like-minded leaders, who share a similar vision and not only work well together, but also love and care about each other, too. How would that enhance your life?

This is not to say that money and success mean nothing at all. Is making money an important part of life? Absolutely. Is part of life producing results? Of course. But there is so much more to life than tangible things. Life is about process. It's about how we produce the results, and who we are when we're producing those results. Remember the movie *Wall Street*? Michael Douglas' character, Gordon Gekko, uttered the infamous line, "The point is, ladies and gentleman, that greed, for lack of a better word, is good." Was he right? Is the never-ending desire to quench your thirst of greed actually good? Well, first of all, an individual's personal definition of *good* is subjective and completely open to interpretation. Ultimately, *good* is judgment with a limitation and a cap on it. Do you want a cap on your financial, emotional, or spiritual profitability?

When I wake up each day, I see incredible possibility, incredible potential in the everyday aspects of life. I see a life with no blinders, no ceiling. What I also see are people who are essentially functioning like the walking dead. You are not a spectator in your life. You are not an extra in a movie. You are not a self-righteous critic and observer. The question you get to ask yourself every morning is, "What difference can I make today? What difference can I make *right now*?"

What would it be like to live a world where *The Walking Dead* isn't a hit TV series? That show is a perfect reflection of what our society has become and what we've settled for. Wouldn't you rather create a world where being alive is celebrated and the act of giving isn't limited to the holiday season? Don't you want to live in a world where we don't have to mark selfless acts on the calendar, relegating them to a certain period of the year? Or even worse, putting them on a bumper sticker: "Honk if you believe in random acts of kindness"? A honk, when used in the right situation, may save a life. But sometimes it is annoying and unnecessary noise, usually meant to be unkind. It shouldn't be used as a meaningless gesture to show support for a cause. Instead of honking in response, why not just be kind in your daily life?

During my thirty years of coaching, I've had the opportunity to work with many extraordinary and powerful people: CEOs, company presidents, business owners, VPs, Fortune 500 companies, etc. One of my longtime clients was a CEO for a financial services company on Wall Street in New York. It was a company specializing in bond trading, and they worked with several of the top financial companies, such as Merrill Lynch, Soloman Brothers, J.P. Morgan, Pimco, Goldman Sachs, Bear Stearns, and others. They made their money by providing trading information. It was a very successful business. My client was making over a million dollars a year and also had an ownership stake in the firm. On paper, he looked like the perfect guy. He lived in a gorgeous home in one of the wealthiest towns in New Jersey. He had a beautiful wife and family. But he admitted to me that he wasn't happy. He knew he wasn't the father he wanted to be to his children. He was not the husband he wanted to be to his wife. He realized that he was ultra-controlling, impatient, and judgmental, with the overwhelming need to always be right. And underneath it all, he was insecure and afraid of losing everything. When he was young, especially during his teenage years, he lacked the confidence he wanted in his social skills, so logically, he focused on studying and hit the books hard. He was motivated by his desire to succeed and his realization that he was very intelligent, but a part of him also wanted to prove all of his critics wrong. To prove himself, to "show them." Because of his internal conflict with his ego, he ended up creating the kind of life everyone dreamed of, a life that would make any parent truly proud, and results that would make most people jealous. Was it what he wanted? Was he happy and satisfied? No.

Deep down inside, he had big visions for his career. He dreamed of starting a new business and selling the one he owned. He found the courage to take that first step. He reached out and hired me to be his coach. Even though he was a financial expert who was brilliant in his work, he was vulnerable and humble enough to acknowledge that he was not perfect and absolutely not where he wanted to be, both professionally and personally.

As I began coaching him, the first aspect of his life we worked on was transforming his attitude, communication habits, and ways of being. Through working together in partnership, I gave him honest, direct, and interruptive feedback. Feedback is information that gives people an opportunity to see, hear, and understand how they show up in the eyes of other people. They are no longer limited to their own experience of themselves. In my work, feedback is essential. People don't hire me to tell them what they want to hear; many of them have employees, family members, and friends who will do just that. Once I had the time to connect with the people in his life, personally and professionally, it was easy to see what was missing and what was not working.

To his credit, he received my feedback with a genuine open-ness and truly embraced it, and thus he began his transformation. We looked at his limiting beliefs, identifying where they came from, how they affected his choices and behaviors, and how he figuratively created this inauthentic version of himself. Through this realization, he was able to let it go. He accessed his heart and changed his previous belief that vulnerability was a weakness to be avoided, and instead began to see vulnerability as a sign of strength. He started leading with his vision, and he developed a new internal mantra: He began to live his life as a vulnerable, loving, and compassionate man. His family life completely trans-formed. The relationship he created with his children was no longer strained, frustrating, and hard. When he changed, they changed. Children are extremely flexible in their behaviors because their beliefs are not yet fully formed. They are like clay, which can be molded and remolded again. When this client first came to me, his marital relationship was on the verge of divorce. He was a workaholic who was disconnected emotionally, and not showing up as a true partner to his wife. When he came home from work, he was often still working, and as a result, wasn't present with the children either. With his personal relationships in breakdown, he committed to making the changes he needed to at home, too. As a result of his redesigning, he and his wife transformed their marriage and created a new level of emotional intimacy. The love light was relit, the passion was present, and the connection was there like never before. They became partners in life. He rede-signed his relationship with his children, getting to know each of them for the first time. In doing so, he realized what an incredible and beautiful gift they were to him. More importantly, he realized how important he was to them as well. From that moment on, his priorities changed. When he was home, he was now *fully present.*

This client also had a vision to start a new business where he would manage the assets of companies and individuals with high net worth. This is called a hedge fund. He declared his vision with me, and we worked together to make it happen. To make this financial vehicle a viable investment for investors but also a worthy business to own, he needed a minimum of fifty million dollars in initial capital. It's a catch-22. No one sees the value in investing in a fund that has no money invested in it. In order to create the investment, my client would need to give presentations to prospective investors, and ultimately, sell himself and his ability. This would require him to develop his communication skills and his powers of public speaking. Not just to speak to people, but to speak to them and also make an impact. As it turns out, he exceeded his initial goal of creating $50,000,000 in capital within five years. Instead, he managed to take it all the way to $3,000,000,000. He accomplished this in less than ten years. He not only surpassed his goal, he took it to a level that he couldn't even imagine. He turned the impossible into the possible.

Here's another anecdote: A woman once approached me to say that she wanted to make her living as a personal coach and trainer, and she asked me to train her. At the time, she worked with the Chamber of Commerce in Dallas and was a business consultant to female business owners. When I first met with her, she did not have the skills to make this dream happen. I hold people to their highest possibilities, and even I couldn't see it at first. She was from Panama, and her English was not very good. She was also very small physically, and showed up timid and insecure. When she spoke, she lacked power, self-esteem, and confidence. I told her that I was willing to work with her to accomplish her goal, but she would have to fully commit to it. She would have to transform her entire being. She would have to show me that she was hungry and that she was serious about her vision. I asked her if she was willing to do whatever it took, and she said yes.

As promised, this slight woman completely *reinvented* herself to become an excellent world-class and world-renowned trainer. She gives workshops and seminars all over the world, particularly in many Spanish-speaking countries. Her English has improved immensely, and as a result, she is even training in the United States. She is a great example of what can happen when people believe in themselves and are willing to fight for what they want. As the artist Pablo Picasso once said, "I am always doing that which I cannot do, in order that I may learn how to do it."

Two other people I've worked with went on to become Ernst & Young Entrepreneur of the Year Award winners. These two clients were already established in their businesses and with a certain level of success, but they were not satisfied. They, too, were hungry to develop themselves and were driven to go where they had never gone before. They were able to reinvent themselves as leaders and entrepreneurs by tapping into their existing potential and turning their weaknesses and blind spots into strengths.

Those of you who are reading this book have that same opportunity to discover not only what's missing, what's in your way, and what's holding you back, but also what's possible for you. Human beings have the capacity to redesign and reinvent their lives. We are the only beings in the entire animal kingdom who have the power to alter the course of our own evolution at this great magnitude.

When I was a child, squirrels gathered nuts, ran around the yard, jumped out of trees, and dodged the cars to avoid becoming road kill. The squirrel has to be one of the most stressed, scared, and nervous animals alive. I would watch these squirrels, amazed and mesmerized at how often they would just miss an oncoming vehicle. They were always frantically scavenging for food, and then desperately dashing back up the tree when a perceived threat emerged. Sometimes I feel like that's how many human beings live. We show up like a bunch of squirrels—spending a majority of our everyday existence doing little but gathering the leftovers of others' inventions, scavenging for our own survival. We settle for mediocrity and scamper around nervously, hoping not to get hit by the world around us, and then we run to take cover and use our remaining energy to protect and defend our prized collection of nuts.

If you examine the everyday life of the squirrel, has it changed since you were a child? Has it altered? I'm fifty years old. Squirrels are still doing the exact same thing today that they were doing fifty years ago. But some human beings aren't. Fifty years ago, we were living in a nuclear world. We were living through the Cold War. We were afraid every day that the U.S. was going to war with the Soviet Union or that they might drop their arsenal of bombs on us. Everyone was paranoid, constantly wondering: "Who's with us? Who's against us?" We were living in a society that bred mistrust, not only globally, but also domestically here in the United States. There were daily protests regarding a variety of causes: women's rights, equality, Vietnam, jobs, gas prices, fair pay for union workers, etc.

Back then, we were living in a world where sending a man to the moon was only a dream. In 1961, John F. Kennedy said, "We are going to put a man on the moon by the end of this decade." This was a perfect demonstration of the power of declaration and responsibility. He knew it would be a challenge and didn't back down to fears of failure and the real possibility that he might look bad. He had a vision, found a purpose, and stood up on the top of the Skinny Branches. Look at his commitment to NASA. Look at the discoveries we've made since then: new worlds, new galaxies, and new technological advances for human beings, which have all been possible because of space exploration and travel. How about what his promise meant to Americans? To the new generations of children who were just being born? When we live our purpose and vision, when we're creating from the space of unbridled and unlimited possibility, we can create anything. We can even create miracles.

It isn't just about the result—it's about the *experience*, that feeling of success and awe, the swell of emotion, and the importance of our values. Those values are consistent with our vision and purpose, and with living on the Skinny Branches of the tree. So declare your inner mantra quietly to yourself, but make sure you also shout it out loud so you can be heard. As the French philosopher Jean Paul-Sartre once said, "Only the guy who isn't rowing has time to rock the boat."

Chapter Three

NEVER CLIP YOUR WINGS

NO ONE CAN REACH the Skinny Branches—the ones that reach high up into the sky and spread far and wide from the safety of the trunk—if they clip their wings. Don't be afraid to fly. Don't be afraid to take chances and risks. Don't stifle your imagination or your creativity. Don't be afraid to soar to new heights. No one can clip your wings unless you let them. This includes your number one critic: YOU. As the German writer Goethe once said, "Magic is believing in yourself. If you can do that, you can make anything happen."

Anatomically speaking, the bumblebee should not be able to fly. Thankfully, it doesn't realize that, and for that reason, it has achieved what should be impossible. Clipping your wings is purely mental; it happens when you listen to the little voices in your mind and give your power away to them. You discourage yourself or others from doing what might be possible simply because it has not been done before. The famous Olympian and marathon runner Roger Bannister ran the first four-minute mile in history—after doctors said the human body could not physically do so. At the time, it was supposedly impossible. Because everyone believed that assessment to be true, other runners "clipped their wings" by not even attempting to break the record. After all, science and research had already said it would be impossible. But Bannister didn't listen. He didn't let anyone clip his wings. He set a world record by being the first man to run a four-minute mile, and others soon followed suit, tying and eventually beating his record.

I believe life is a team sport, starting from the very beginning, the conception of you. There you were minding your own business, a spirit floating somewhere in the universe, when your parents said, "Hey baby, tonight's the night." They made love, and a seed was planted. It may not have happened exactly this way, but you get the idea. Whether it was a conscious decision on their part or not, they chose to create life. And nine months later, you were born into the world. We were all created from this very basic intimate relationship. The relationships you create with your parents have the single greatest impact on your experience in life, and ultimately, on your future.

Imagine this: We could be living in a society where the eighteen-year-old children in this country grow into adults who are responsible, loving, and committed—passionate leaders with high integrity. They could care about their success, their friends' success, and their society's success. If this happened, we would actually be able to transform the culture that we live in. What we're producing instead is the opposite of that. Let's look at some of the ways we are clipping each other's wings.

We're tolerating an education system that is ranked 17th in the world. Can you believe that the U.S., which has arguably the most effective democracy in the world, is home to an education system that is ranked 17th? How is that even possible? We're involved in multiple wars and conflicts in Syria, Afghanistan, Iraq, and virtually the entire Middle East. We're directly involved in the challenging negotiations with Iran in order to stop them from producing nuclear weapons. We're putting the lives of young men and women at risk in order to stand up for the rights of other people throughout the world. We are putting our own children in harm's way. Imagine if we lived in a society where peace was not something to aspire to, but where peace, unity, and prosperity were already a way of life. In this society, love would be a way of life. Relationships would be healthy. Women would be safe. Children would have the opportunity to live with passion and freedom, not just survive in fear.

In the United States right now, almost 50% of marriages end in divorce. The result is that people are more hesitant, skeptical and cynical about whether marital unions can work or are even worth it to begin with. Over the last thirty years, I've coached hundreds of thousands of people, many of whom are married. Many others were married at one time, but are now divorced. In my professional opinion, no more than 10% or 15% of these still-married couples are happily married. The 85% who are married and unhappy will make excuses, justifications, rationalizations. They'll say, "I'm staying married for the children. I'm staying married because I gave my word. I'm staying married because I believe in God and my interpretation of God says divorce is bad and wrong. I'm staying married because I'm afraid to be alone. I'm staying married because of financial security. I'm staying married because it will really hurt my parents if I get divorced." Some are still married because she looks at him and thinks, "Well, I could do worse. At least he has a pulse." Or maybe he realizes that she cooks and does the chores in the house. He realizes that she's basically a good person, so he thinks, "This isn't what I want, but it's okay, so I'm going to stay. I guess it's better than being alone." It has been estimated that approximately 40% of marriages are marred by infidelity from either one or both partners. Clearly something is missing in most marriages.

A very low percentage of the married couples I meet are, in my opinion, in love. When I say "in love," I'm referring to couples who look forward not only to spending the rest of their lives together, but to creating an extraordinary life together. I'm talking about the kind of relationship where you can see and feel their love when you are in close proximity. It's like a magical experience—the energy is flowing, the connection is natural, the respect is present, and the love is palpable.

Unfortunately, I see very few examples of this type of relationship on the golf course. Whenever we're finished playing, so many of the married men will hang around in the bar to drink with the other guys. There is no sense of urgency or desire to get home. They all want to stay at the club as long as possible. Rarely do I hear anyone calling home to talk to their wives, and when I do, I almost never hear the words "I love you." Me? I can't wait to get home. I can't wait to get home to see my wife, to see my kids, to be in their lives: go to that recital, go to cheerleading, go to their sporting events, listen to stories about their days, help them with tough homework. I love my life. If we don't clip people's wings, we can produce a society full of people who care about themselves and others.

Today, obesity is one of the biggest issues we face in America. In the United States, obesity has become a multibillion-dollar business. Our country is the most obese nation in the world. We don't just eat. We stuff ourselves like piñatas. We eat unhealthily. Why don't we take care of ourselves? It doesn't start with the food. It starts with our mentality, our attitudes. We're eating to numb, avoid, or pacify our pain. Our mothers and fathers are also eating to medicate and cope with pain they have held within from their own past history—pain they are now passing onto their children. The result is, we are creating a society of pain, suffering, and victimization, and then we are passing it to the following generations.

If we stopped clipping other people's wings, we would see a major decline in bullying. Right now, bullying is a very big and dangerous problem in our schools. I thought bullying was bad when I was a kid. It seems so much worse now than it was forty years ago. Social media outlets, such as Facebook, Twitter, Instagram, and Snapchat, make cyberbullying easier than ever with the simple push of a button. There are so many ways to punish kids, to make them feel wrong, to shame them, to make them feel horrible about themselves. When I was a kid, fights would be resolved with fists after school. I'm not saying that that was any better or any healthier, because we were clipping wings back then, too. I'm just saying that we're perpetuating and fostering a society full of violence and fear. Young girls and boys are afraid to go to school. They're worried about how they look, about what people are posting about them from behind a computer screen, about how many friends they have on Facebook, and about whether or not embarrassing and scandalous photos of them are being uploaded for everyone to see.

Teenagers are committing suicide with alarming frequency. When I was a child, I didn't know one person who tried to take his own life. I grew up in Boston and attended a large high school with over 2,000 students. Ending your life wasn't an option people discussed, no matter how difficult the challenges we faced were, either at home or in the hallways of our school. Today, it has unfortunately become very common to hear of a teenager committing suicide. It happens almost daily, and then it is publicized on every news channel. Teenage suicide has increased 25% over the last twenty-five years in the United States. Too often, it happens as a result of relentless bullying, not only from adults but also from other children, clipping other children's wings. Clearly, we need to do a much better job as parents in raising our children. Maybe the most important aspect is developing our ability to relate to them, to connect. We shouldn't just teach, scold, and discipline.

We're also seeing gun violence like never before, not only in our society at large, but also in our schools. Remember the tragedy that occurred sixteen years ago at Columbine High School in Littleton, Colorado? When it happened, our entire nation wept. I wept. It wasn't the first act of violence in America, but it marked the first act of its kind in a school. We were rocked to the core of our being. We were scared and fearful of why it happened, or how it could happen, or if it would happen again. If it could happen in a middle-class, suburban town like Littleton, why couldn't it happen to our own children? Shouldn't they be safe in their classrooms and schools? It was revealed that the two murderers collected weapons and ammunition, preparing for their attack in their parents' garage. When the parents were asked what they knew about it, they said they were unaware. How is it possible, as a parent, to have a fully-loaded armory in your garage and not know anything about it? That makes no sense. That is, until we look deeper into the root cause of this dangerous behavior. We're seeing the damage that children are doing to other children because of issues in their home life. Whether those issues are parental divorce, domestic violence, alcoholism, emotional abuse, poverty, financial distress, lack of communication, lack of love, lack of connection, or other forms of dysfunction, the result is a society which has become an accurate reflection of our broken homes and strained family life. Our wings are clipped and we want revenge. We want others to suffer, to feel the enormous pain we feel. We clip wings in hopes of getting some kind of relief or satisfaction in return. But we wind up feeling empty, and sometimes, worse.

This comes down to the simple theory of *cause and effect*. Long ago, the Greek philosopher Aristotle noticed that things don't just happen randomly—they essentially happen for a reason. Most of us look out at the world and see it as it is, then give up or resign ourselves to the evidence we see on the surface. We don't take the time to use our amazing intelligence in order to discover the source of "what is." In our society, we've even coined one of the most pathetic phrases of defeat in the English language: "It is what it is." This is most often said as a form of cynical resignation versus acceptance, the latter of which would give us power and choice.

Take a minute to imagine if we created and lived in a society where people actually cared about themselves and about the quality of their lives. A society where people believed in their dreams, their visions, and their purposes. This level of caring would surely show up in the way we care for other people. Maybe, in the beginning, we couldn't put a complete end to bullying, but at least we could empower children to stand up and let their voices be heard, to make a difference for other kids in need of support. Some children who are bullied have trust issues, are insecure, and doubt themselves. But imagine what would be possible if the others reached out and stepped up to empower them? This could result in higher levels of confidence, greater participation, better attitudes, more desire to excel in classwork, and a greater sense of security for our schools and our children.

We could be living in a society where nobody wins unless *everybody wins*. Instead, we now live in a society where everybody is looking to advance their own agenda. It's every man for himself. The game is survival of the fittest, and it's been around since the beginning of recorded time. How's it working out so far? Who's really winning in the game of survival? Any win you achieve at the expense of someone else's self-esteem, dignity, or life, diminishes the win itself. You'll always know, deep down inside, where your authenticity lives, whether you won with integrity or not.

The current culture and environment we live in doesn't create the space for strong, trusting relationships. Every door in every neighborhood is double- and triple- and quadruple-locked with dead bolts. We use security systems and alarms. We are armed to the hilt. Americans have an estimated 300 million guns. Texas just passed open carry legislation. We are afraid to go outside, and constantly worry about where our children are at all times. Instead of talking to our neighbors, we drive our gigantic SUVs directly into our garages. We don't even know who lives next to us.

What would be possible if we stopped clipping our wings and the wings of others? What kind of community could we live in? What could we create? Can you imagine an environment where we wake up in the mornings, open our doors, and go outside to actually talk to and connect with our neighbors, and our surrounding neighborhood? Imagine an environment where we're not worried about locking our doors anymore. Instead, we build trust and create a community with the people who live near us. Imagine celebrating holidays together, creating fun and safe block parties, during which all the children could play and interact as brothers and sisters. In this world, if you needed to borrow some sugar, you could send your son to the house next door and he would come back with not only sugar, but fresh baked cookies, too. Imagine creating a society where we care about one another, are working together, and are in it for each other. There's a certain level of trust and humanity. It's not only civilized—it's a civilization. As the old African proverb states, "It takes a village to raise a child."

Other countries do not see the same disheartening statistics that we do. In the United States right now, the Centers for Disease Control (CDC) estimates that 1 in every 4 girls and 1 in every 6 boys will be sexually abused before the age of 18. These numbers only include cases that are reported; many more go unreported. It is estimated that there are over 42 million victims of sexual abuse in America today. And this statistic doesn't even include physical, mental, verbal, or emotional abuse.

In my trainings, I often ask if any of the students have ever been physically, mentally, verbally, or emotionally abused, and usually 90% of the hands in the room go up. We are clipping the wings of our children by beating them: beating them with our hands, beating them with our fists, beating them with our magazines, our belts, our straps, beating them with a switch. We will actually ask our children to go outside and pull the switch off the tree. Is this acceptable? Do these sound like the results and actions of the greatest country on Earth? If asked, any decent American would say that this is totally unacceptable, that we will not tolerate this. I hate to say it, but based on our results, we do tolerate it. There are other societies where sexual abuse is an anomaly. It's a shock and virtually unheard of. In our society, it's part of daily life. And those are just the cases we're aware of.

What can you do about it? How can you stop clipping other people's wings? A powerful way to stop clipping their wings is to infuse them with vision and a sense of purpose. A vision and sense of purpose that will give them the opportunity to share their beautiful gifts with the world around them—to not only see the beauty in others, but to hold them accountable for bringing this beauty to life. Remember this question from the Bible: "Am I my brother's keeper?" The short answer is YES! We must give love, compassion, and understanding to people, and we must do it now, urgently. We must use our power in a constructive way. To communicate thoughts, concepts, strategies, and ideas that move people forward. The lives of others are literally, and figuratively, at stake.

If we stopped clipping the wings, we could create an ideal society. Ask yourself: Why are we having children? What is our vision for our children? How can we become the parents that our parents weren't for us? What kind of people do we want to be? How do we develop ourselves as parents? How can we be examples for our children, the wind beneath their wings?

Imagine if instead of clipping wings, we became the wind beneath the wings of our husbands and our wives. For example, you could start by trying not to tear into your husband for all the things he doesn't do as soon as he comes home. Maybe you're emotionally frustrated because of your choice to abandon the career you wanted while your husband gets to pursue his. But maybe he's giving it his all, working hard, making money, and doing whatever it takes to provide for you and the family. What if you put aside your disappointment or boredom when he comes in after a long day? Instead of clipping his wings by focusing on the fact that he didn't take out the garbage as he promised, show up at the door as he arrives, grab him passionately in your arms, and say, "Honey, I'm so proud of you. I love you. You are my man, my hero. You are the rock in this family." Can you imagine the look on his face? I guarantee you, he will be out of his body and so happy to be home. Is there a time to talk about the garbage? Of course! But why does it have to be the first thing you say? Can you become aware of your ego conversations and limiting voices in time to interrupt yourself, to focus on him and what he wants or needs?

On the flip side, maybe you know your wife wants your help with the chores, but she never asks. She doesn't ask because she thinks you don't care and don't want to contribute. Instead of waiting for her to ask, instead of selfishly acting like a prince, here's what you do: Get up as soon as the dinner is over. Make sure she stays seated, and tell her to relax. You can even take her over to the couch and give her the remote. You tell her to put on any show that she wants to watch, and as soon as you complete the dishes, you'll be there to connect with her and watch whatever she's selected. You're showing her how much you love her and how much you care by doing something that she would normally be doing. Most importantly, it's the way you're doing it, in the spirit of contribution. This is not just an act of love. It's also a conscious decision not to clip her wings. What are the advantages of this? First of all, she will feel loved and appreciated, and know that you are on her team, that you are her partner. It becomes more than a simple gesture. She's not only going to feel love, she's going to experience the feeling of being *in* love. And she's going to be in love with *you*, not with the pool guy from *Sex in the City*. Why? Because you were the wind beneath her wings.

So don't spend a majority of your precious time looking for what's wrong, what's missing, and what's not working. Instead, we need to focus our energy, creativity, and power on what we want, the possibilities that exist in our lives. Change is possible, whether we make a difference in the way we raise our children, the way we participate in our romantic relationships, or the way we interact with our families. How about not clipping the wings?

Let's say your daughter got a "B" on an important exam. She's not a failure just because she got a "B." Yes, it may not be excellent—like getting an "A"—but a "B" is nothing close to a disaster. Now imagine sitting down with her, to support her and take her under your wing. Let her know how much you love and care about her performing to the best of her abilities. Is there anything wrong with that? No, of course not. Help her figure out how to improve her grade from a "B" to an "A," and most importantly, help her realize the value of achieving it. What would it take from her? What would she need to do differently? What are the ways you can support her?

Here's an example from my own life: My daughter Savannah once failed her math class in the final semester of ninth grade. Before the next school year started, I sat down with her and said, "Babe, this is a new year with new opportunities and new possibilities. Everything you've done prior to now won't matter if you can get back on track. So my first question to you is, what kind of grades are acceptable to you, and why? How important is it for you to get your math studies back on track? I asked her this in a loving, supportive, and non-judgmental way.

She talked to me about her vision for her future, including some of the careers and jobs she might want to pursue. One of them was being a sports journalist, either a writer or broadcaster. We talked about the different colleges that offered a journalism major, schools that she might aspire to apply to in the future. We talked about the grades she would need to get in order for these colleges to be an option for her. I asked her, "How do you think you'd feel about yourself if you turned your math grade around and gave yourself the opportunity to pursue journalism?" Her face lit up with genuine excitement, enthusiasm, and confidence. It was as if, in that moment, she could visualize her future experiences and the way they would make her feel, as if they had already happened. Now there's a powerful concept for you to think about. I want you to do what my daughter did that day—imagine yourself standing in the future, as if it's already happened and you're looking back at the present. What do you see for yourself? How is it different from what you have now?

That day, Savannah and I created a comprehensive plan detailing how she was going to achieve her vision for herself and for her own happiness, not for her mom's or dad's. She was going to study, do her homework every day, and double-check the homework before class the next day. She was no longer going to be satisfied with simply completing a test, just getting through it. Savannah's new intention was to review her answers and check her work. She also committed to achieving the highest possible grades in all of her classes, to not only improve in that one subject.

Then I asked her, "How can I support you? What can I do? You're my daughter and I love you. If you don't win, I don't win. We're in this together." And she gave me a thorough answer. "I'd like to talk to you everyday about it," she said. "I want you to remind me to do my homework because you know sometimes I get spacey, and sometimes even lazy. And I'd like you to support me if I don't understand something."

So I said, "Absolutely. I will do everything you're asking me to do. I will stand by you every step of the way."

Just like that, our joint commitment to her schoolwork became the equivalent of a partnership, a team. My daughter's attitude and confidence were transformed by the end of the conversation, and of course, she had an excellent start to school. She created A's and B's in her math class the entire year, ending up with a "B" average, exactly what she'd wanted. This was the same girl who'd received an "F" the previous year, who'd convinced herself that she wasn't smart enough to be good at math. Her self-esteem had taken a major hit as a result. Her grades from the year before were not acceptable for a person who intends to go to college, and she felt horrible about herself because of it. She was convinced that it meant she wasn't capable. The day we had our conversation, we were able to interrupt her painful experience and limiting beliefs through my coaching, and by making a conscious effort not to clip her wings. Instead, we worked together.

Too often, parents expect their children to manage things on their own, especially when they become teenagers. It's very important to support our children as they begin spreading their wings to fly, but it's a learning process. It is not our job as parents to become the judge, jury, and executioner of our children's dreams. We can create many advantages for ourselves and for them if we learn to become the wind beneath their wings.

Challenges will always arise. The world will throw us curve balls. There will always be a cynic out there, someone who says it can't be done, and it isn't possible. You say you're in love, and women will say, "All men are dogs, they only want one thing." When you say you're going to be a rich, famous, and successful entrepreneur someday, some friends may be jealous, or may simply underestimate you, and will say, "You're not good enough, and it'll never happen." Whatever it is, somebody will always be out there to challenge your dreams and visions, to tell you that what you want isn't possible. The French writer and philosopher Voltaire once said, "It is difficult to free fools from the chains they revere." Some people simply love to be right about what can't be done. What a shame, and what a waste of energy.

The opposite of clipping people's wings is instilling in them the belief and confidence to rise up in any and all situations, no matter the challenges and obstacles they face. In doing so, they can turn obstacles into opportunities, breakdowns into breakthroughs, and lemons into lemonade. It's a matter of having the power, the confidence, and the belief in yourself to see it through. Imagine telling your employees, "Hey, wait a minute! I'm the boss. You do what I say, not what I do. I don't want to hear your opinions." Even if you don't like or agree with an employee's idea, you should find another way to respond to their communication. Do you want a company of yes-men? Do you want a company of followers, of people who are always waiting for the instructions? Even if someone has a weak idea, at least they made an attempt to contribute by displaying courage in sharing a proposal. If you don't think the proposal is going to work, you should never clip the wings. You never stifle the contribution, the leadership, the responsibility, or the courage. You might say, "I think we need to do it this way," or "Here's where I think we should focus," or "Here's why I think we should spend this money." But you should always acknowledge the contributions from your employees. Sometimes you say yes, even if you don't think their suggestion is the best option. Of course, you always tell them why you think it won't work. Be honest. But if they're passionate and adamant, if they're convinced their idea or plan is going work, and are committed to seeing it through, then sometimes you let go of your point of view. You say, "This is your decision. I will back you 100%. But understand the risks. Make it work. Let's go!" Do you sit back cynically waiting for failure? No, you stand with them and make yourself available for any needed coaching, strategizing, and support. Always back up your employees, your teams. How you personally think it should be done is one thing, but sometimes you must allow people the space to figure it out for themselves. One way to encourage and motivate employees is to remind them of who they are. Remind them that they have the power to create anything that they want in their lives. Give them space to express themselves, their ideas, and their suggestions. Remember, people don't always need to be agreed with, but they really need to be heard and respected.

In business, thinking like an entrepreneur is a powerful way to avoid clipping anyone's wings. Entrepreneurs live outside of the box. They don't just pop out of the box once in a while—they actually live outside of the box, at all times. To an entrepreneur, what isn't is always more important than what is. An entrepreneur is invested in the future. Behind the scenes, Apple is always at least two to three generations ahead of the products they are currently selling. They live ahead of the wave, ahead of the curve. Apple understands better than most that what isn't is more important than what is. They are 100% invested in an unprecedented, undiscovered future. To an entrepreneur, there is no such thing as a bad or stupid idea. Imagine creating a culture of creativity in your business. What would be possible?

Let's take another look at our relationships outside of work. Love is an action verb, and love is not passive. In a loving relationship, love has many faces. Sometimes love is alive and vibrant, like a passionate energy force that flows through your body and wants to connect with your partner. Sometimes, love is about forgiving, letting go of frustration, being patient, allowing the other person space to manage something that is bothering them from work, even if it is interfering with previous plans. The one constant in love is that love is not constant.

If you declare today that you're going to strengthen your connection with your wife, or that you're going to create a sexy and intimate experience with your lover, then you are now committed and have the responsibility of seeing it through. It's no longer just a nice idea or a concept or a thought. Now, it's a declaration. You're on the Skinny Branch of the tree. "Today, I am committed to creating intimacy with my lover. I am committed to creating love, passion, and fun for my husband." You can make this commitment even if you haven't experienced this love connection in days, weeks, months, or years. Is it possible? Yes, as long as you believe that no one can clip your wings. The author Richard Bach once said, "True love stories never have endings." If we are the wind beneath the wings, love doesn't die. Instead, it evolves, just as a caterpillar transforms into a butterfly with unique, *majestic colors.*

You may not love baseball, or even enjoy watching baseball on TV, but let's imagine your husband loves the Boston Red Sox.

Without him asking or knowing, you look up what time the game starts and put on all your sexy Red Sox gear, because you know that once he sees you in that outfit, he's going to know that you love and care about him. He will know that his passions matter to you, too. Your actions show that you're thinking about him and what's important to him. Can you imagine the reaction that your husband will have as he's turning on the game? Imagine his response—and more importantly, your own experience—knowing the connection you have created together. He might now open his heart to you in a whole new way, in a way he hasn't for a long time. It's a small thing to the average person, but take a moment to imagine what it would mean to him because of how important this team and this game is. For many fans, it's a lifelong passion that began during childhood.

Now let's say you're at CVS. It's not Valentine's Day, or your wife's birthday, or Mother's Day, or anything like that. It's just an ordinary day. You're at CVS running errands, buying some day-to-day necessities. While at CVS, even though you're in a rush, you stop and read through the greeting cards until you find the perfect one with a message that speaks to how special your wife is to you. You visualize in your mind how much you love her, how much she does for the kids and the whole family. You make time, even though you didn't think you had it, to look for something that is unique, something that's special, not just one of the typical Hallmark cards. It's a simple act that shows effort, caring, and sensitivity at the same time. Small gifts like that don't have to be expensive or elaborate, but they can show your wife how special she is to you. When you take the time to pick something out, you create an affirmation of your love for her. You move out of the temporary state of Eros, erotic love, and move into the beautiful state of unfolding what can truly be created in your daily love life—a deep, profound, and soulful love. This is possible with *conscious thought and action.*

Many of you come from or have blended families. Even if, biologically speaking, the children are not your own, you can still create a loving, connected, and influential relationship with them. As an example, I have three stepchildren: Andrew, Haley, and Conner. The key here is to never, under any circumstances, see them, interact with them, or hold them as your *stepchildren*. This is something I thank my dad, Bob, for teaching me, not only with his words, but with his behaviors and actions. He has always treated Larry and me as if we were his own. I love each of my children individually. They are unique, and I relate and connect to each one differently.

Let's begin with Andrew. Andrew is very smart, and boy, does he know it. I have worked hard to develop a level of trust with him, so he knows that I genuinely care. Over time, he has really opened up to me and isn't afraid to talk about virtually any subject, including girls and his feelings or insecurities. Even though he's a teenager and sometimes experiences the typical adolescent grumpiness, he and I relate on a wide range of topics and show affection through talking, communication, and dialogue. From sports, to politics, to business, to world events, he is interested in learning and discovering his own point of view. He also has a fantastic sense of humor, and I love it when he just lets loose. Sometimes, he'll start singing, dancing, and making crazy facial expressions. For him to do that in front of Hillary and me means he feels safe to be himself, knowing he won't be judged, knowing that he's loved. It took him a while, but he now openly says "I love you" to me.

Next we have my eleven-year-old, Haley, who loves music, Instagram, the Disney Channel, fashion, and her friends. Now, imagine how our relationship would be if I chose to only talk to her about sports and politics. Do you think she'd want to open up to me? Do you think she would feel like I really understand her, that I care? It can't always be about you, *your* wants and *your* priorities. Yes, you are the parent, the "boss," but the title doesn't create the relationship or the connection. I create a connection with her by not only being interested in the things that interest her, but also being sensitive to her emotions, which run HIGH, 24/7. Sometimes I'll sit down and ask her to play one of her favorite songs. I will even sing along with her, to show her that I care, and also to show her that my willingness to sing doesn't have anything to do with whether I can sing well. Would it really hurt or injure you that badly to listen to the latest Ariana Grande song? I'm confident you'll get through it just fine. But what you won't be able to get through is her completely shutting you out because she doesn't get the sense that you understand her.

This leads me to Conner. He is super outrageous, high-energy, and very bright. He loves to play games and make things, and is always inventing new ways to experience life. We talk about topics of interest to him: school, soccer, friends, animals, what he wants to be when he grows up. Spending time with Conner always requires our full attention. Why? Because he is like a Cirque du Soleil show. There is never a dull moment when Conner's around. One of the main ways I've been able to develop an excellent relationship with Conner is by showing him that I love him and value his thoughts. He's the youngest, and it's not easy for him, with big shoes to fill. Sometimes, he feels like he gets the least amount of quality time, so Hillary and I are sensitive to making sure he feels important and special. Because he knows I care about him, I've been able to introduce him to rock and roll music, and have begun what I like to call "The Edumacation of Conner." It's a word I invented that is essentially short for "education of music." We don't just listen to any and all music, but what I call Michael's Essentials. We mix it up: Flight of the Conchords, Beastie Boys, B-52's, Led Zeppelin... Well, you get the idea. Balance is essential when trying not to clip the wings.

To avoid clipping the wings of your children, you need to relate to them on their level, connect with them, meet them where they are. Don't only play rock and roll when you're with your daughter if that's not what she wants to listen to. Instead, find out when her favorite artist is coming to town and take her to the concert. Can you imagine how cool you would become in her eyes if you were the one to introduce her to the latest hot jam? Play it on the way to cheerleading or to a recital. Sing out loud, whether you can carry a tune or not. Encourage her to sing along with you; she'll think you're a "beast." (But definitely, do *not* sing in front of her friends. That's pushing it.) Your active participation will go a long way in creating the connection that will help her fly and soar. How about playing a video game? It doesn't matter if you are good at it, just the act of playing and taking an interest will make the difference. At least make an effort to watch without clipping the wings by making critical statements, such as, "This is stupid. I can't believe you're wasting your time rotting your brains," and so on. You can get over your aversion to video games, but you won't be able to get over being disconnected from and completely out of a relationship with your children.

With employees at work, take time to acknowledge, on a regular basis, two or three things that each person is doing well. You can't only focus on your list of things that are not working, or things that need to be improved. If there isn't a balance between what's working and what's not working, then the person will feel as if you're only concentrating on the negative side all the time. They will be disempowered, and if they're disempowered, how well can they perform their jobs and tasks? What price will you and your company pay? Think of the mistakes you've made in your past employee relationships that led to even bigger breakdowns beyond one individual's job performance.

If you're an entrepreneur who is about to start, or has recently started, a business, your first objective is to create the vision of the company. Often, in the early stages, the financial data—such as cash flow and capital—will drive the decisions you make. Cash flow and capital expenditures are essential, but you need to develop a solid business plan. You need to figure out how you'll generate business, attract customers, create marketing opportunities, build relationships, and establish credibility. Usually, this requires an investment, and obviously investment is congruent with risk. As entrepreneurs, we accept and embrace risk, but not necessarily blind risks. Certainly, doing your research and homework is essential to success. Smart risks are backed by analytical thought, logic, and critical thinking. If you're vision-driven and confident, you can take risks with passion and aggressiveness. You've got to marry those concepts together. You can't allow your fear and desperation to control your decisions. You shouldn't leave it up to chance and dwell on the worst-case scenarios. *Entrepreneurs never clip their own wings.*

When you put money into a business, it could be viewed as debt, and in a sense, it is. But it also could be viewed as an investment. Buying or investing in something is like planting a seed or crop, and often, it's hard to see progress immediately. The nature of investing is the idea that your money will grow and expand, and eventually the business will become profitable over time. Any business owner or entrepreneur understands that there is a certain degree of risk in any venture, but as long as the risks you take are consistent with the vision of your business, then the expectation is that eventually, with proper strategy, the crops will flourish and profit will roll in. The most successful entrepreneurs are up at dawn, working out their minds and bodies, getting themselves ready to create each and every day. Imagine asking yourself daily, "What am I doing today to make my business successful? What am I committed to creating today—or this week, or by Friday at 6 o'clock—that will help move the figurative ball towards the goal line?"

When coaching people, I always ask two very important questions: "How many?" and "By when?" By answering those questions, you put yourself in a game of accountability every day, and that will assist you in creating benchmarks towards achieving your ultimate vision and the success of your business.

As an entrepreneur, one of your biggest priorities is to surround yourself with a championship team. To be successful, you want to be excellent at everything you do. You are not perfect, and you're certainly not a master of all things. The ability to be honest with yourself about your own skills, talents, and abilities, is essential in determining what to look for in other people. Most businesses are not a one-woman operation. They require the expertise, commitment, dedication, and skills of several different contributors. Ideally, each member will add his or her special ingredient to help make the venture a success, not only during the launch of a start-up, but also in establishing a platform for future expansion of existing companies. Acknowledging your weaknesses and challenges is not clipping your wings. It's a sign of strength of character and confidence in the vision and success of your endeavor.

Once you clearly identify who you are and who you are not, then you can surround yourself with people who make up for the qualities that you still lack. You're building a championship team, person by person. Imagine what would happen if your core team, the founders, all had the same skills and personality styles. Imagine if they were also all deficient in areas that are necessary for the business succeed. What do you see when you look at your core team? You need to make sure that every skill you need is met by at least one person. Only then will you be able to move the business onto a successful path toward the future.

Now ask yourself what you can do today to ensure that this business is on track with your vision. Who can you hire, who can you work with, or how can you surround yourself with the kind of people needed to make the business successful? Once you've assembled this group of all-stars, what are the first steps you should take to make sure you're aligned in the vision? What can you do to transform the vision of this business into reality? What values are consistent with making that happen? How large is the gap between where you are and the implementation of this business success? What is that gap specifically? Where are you lacking focus? Where are you not getting the job done at the level that you need to? Where are the company wings being clipped? And who is clipping the wings?

Business people are often victims of circumstance, victims of the economy or the stock market, victims of competitors, and victims of poor preparation, underestimating expenses, or over-estimating financial success. Knowing that, how can you go after your vision, go after your business in a whole new way? What stories, excuses, or justifications would you have to give up? What would it take to redesign yourself as a leader? As a team? As an organization? In both your life and your relationships, don't let others clip your wings, don't clip your own wings, and don't clip the wings of the people around you. You'll need those wings to get out on the Skinny Branches.

But what happens if someone tries to clip your wings? Remember, you will always cross paths with a cynic, or with somebody out there who is fearful or has their own limiting beliefs due to their own past experiences. Unfortunately, the culture of the world we live in today is similar to the story of the sand crabs. In the story, every time one of the crabs tries to break free and go out on its own, the mass of crabs reaches out to pull it back in. It's such a sure thing that you could even place the crabs in a bucket with no lid and not have to worry that they might escape. Often, what stops people from celebrating the success of others, is their disappointment with the life they've chosen. The key point here is that they were the ones who chose it. They had a choice and made the choice.

It's important to be conscious and aware that people will give us negative feedback and criticism, whether solicited or not. The bigger the game you play, the more you will be challenged. You have to learn to listen without giving away your power. If somebody makes an observation or comment about you, is it automatically true? Sometimes yes, and sometimes no. What if they're just looking for a reaction? Maybe their intention is knocking you down a peg or simply getting a rise out of you. Often, we react exactly the way these instigators want. Maybe what they're saying is just an opinion, their point of view, their interpretation. But this might also be an opportunity for you to examine the situation objectively and make sure you're not coming across in a destructive or ineffective way. Maybe it was the way you communicated your thoughts, or the tone of voice you used, or even your perceived attitude. If you *own your thoughts*, no one can clip your wings.

As human beings, we constantly receive feedback and new information from people around us, and all too often, we sell out to the majority opinion and simply fitting in. I went to a business dinner the other night with my wife. Before we went, I asked her if she knew what they were serving, knowing that I am on a special diet and no longer eat red meat. Yes, I live in Texas, the steak capital of the world. I started to worry that this might become an awkward situation, given that it is common to serve meat at such events. I said to my wife, "Babe, I want you to know, I'll refuse to eat red meat if they serve it. Do you think they'll be serving vegan burgers?" I was half-joking, but I really started thinking about it. What would I do if I were in a situation where everyone is sitting at this big table where steak is being served, and I'm the only one who isn't eating it? How would I handle the situation? The discomfort of not going with the crowd? What would I do to keep my integrity intact while staying true to my vision for my health? I didn't want the hosts or the guests to feel like they were being judged by me, nor did I want to bring unnecessary attention to myself and my eating restrictions.

In order to create a life worth living, I need to be ALIVE to create it. I actually love the taste of red meat. What I don't love is how I feel after eating it, and how it adversely affects my body. One of the challenges I faced when turning fifty years old was knowing that my body had changed over the past three decades. Thirty years ago, I could eat steak five days in a row and then polish off hamburgers on the other two days. At the time, it didn't adversely affect me in any way that I could see or feel. I had no problems digesting my food. But now, my body has changed. Over the last few years, I've noticed that each time I eat any kind of red meat, my digestive system responds negatively.

I made a conscious choice to live healthily in order to create the quality of life that I truly want. That's why I'm choosing food that is easier to digest, even though it may not be what I crave or desire. As for how that dinner worked out, they ended up serving chicken. Phew! It all worked out fine in the end. I had decided to stand up for my commitment and my health, regardless of how uncomfortable it would make me or the other guests feel. Even though it would have been difficult for me to risk disapproval, ridicule, or judgment, it was important for me to follow through on my vision and values. Certainly, I would have communicated my decision in a respectful way. The choice I was making had nothing to do with my opinion about them or their choices.

When we change the way we live, not only does it affect us, but it can have a major impact on others as well. This is even true when it comes to small, everyday choices like our eating habits. Maybe someone else at the dinner would have said, "I'm so glad you have chosen not to eat the meat and are sticking to your dietary needs. Good for you." Maybe nothing would have been said at all. Maybe it was only a big deal to me and no one else. Or maybe I would have inspired someone else to reconsider their own health, diet and food choices. How many times have you clipped your own wings by thinking something would be so much worse than it actually turned out to be? How many times have you talked yourself into fears that don't exist externally? Think of all the time you wasted worrying about *imaginary foes and critics.*

It all comes down to the power of interpretation. If we can remind ourselves, particularly in times of crisis or stress, to use our minds and not let our minds use us, then wow, we're entering a whole new level of awareness. We're expanding our choices. You have the power to interpret all information and feedback the way you choose. If you're on an airplane that's flying through rough turbulence due to bad weather, do you have to be afraid? Do you have to hold on for dear life and try to control the plane by leaning in one direction or the other? Do you have to take out your sacred book of scriptures and start reading passages for fear that you may not make it, that this could be the end of your life? Can you experience turbulence on a plane without clipping your wings or the wings of the plane?

What if you choose to let go, to throw your hands above your head like you're on a roller coaster and say, "Whoa, here we go, bring it on; I love turbulence! This is fantastic; it's like being on a roller coaster!"? You can embrace it. Everybody has a choice in how they interpret information. When you're stuck in traffic, do you have to be angry? Do you need to automatically go into road rage mode? Do you immediately assume the world is out to get you? No, you can actually roll down your windows, turn up the volume on your favorite U2 song, and sing out loud, maybe even get the people around you to sing along. What might happen if you did? Think of the empowering energy you could bring to the environment around you, even in traffic. You always have a choice.

In our relationships, in society, and in this world, feedback is always being provided, sometimes with our permission, and sometimes without our permission. You should always check the source of the information. You are in charge of how you hear the feedback and how you respond or react to it. Do you want to go through your life being arrogant, ego-driven, and self-righteous? Do you want to be that person who thinks he already knows everything? That person who won't listen to or embrace helpful feedback just because he doesn't like the way it was delivered or because the other person was being insensitive? The ability to listen to feedback—and use it to help us redesign our lives—is a valuable skill. It will not clip our wings. If anything, it can make us more aerodynamic.

In my professional opinion, the most successful people in the world are not just open to feedback—they seek it and demand it. They expect their closest friends and family, or the people they work with, to be honest with them about what's working and what isn't. How does anyone really know if they're on track in life? Do we know because we listen to our egos? No, our egos will always tell us that our problems in life, no matter how big or how small, are someone else's responsibility. Our culture reinforces the victim mentality that is prevalent today. Just watch the news on TV. When was the last time you saw a broadcast dedicated to what's working in the world, the generosity and kindness of people, the abundant possibilities for the future?

Today, the television market is saturated with "reality" TV. In other words, people placed under manufactured stress and pressure—ashamed, embarrassed, and in chaos, until the torch is finally smothered and they're voted off the island. In so many ways, this description sadly captures our current living condition.

I believe life is always an opportunity for learning. Not learning as in receiving information from people who "know" all the answers, and then regurgitating that information in the form of a right-or-wrong exam. I'm talking about experiencing life and truly absorbing its lessons. This brings me to one of my passions in life, golf. In my thirty-seven years of playing, I have never even come close to the level of Jack Nicklaus, Tiger Woods, Phil Mickelson, or any of the other great golfers out there—but I'm a pretty good amateur. I'm a single-digit handicap. At one time in my early thirties, I even got down to a 1.0 handicap. One of the aspects I love most about golf is the never-ending opportunity to go from breakdown to breakthrough. Wash, rinse, dry, repeat. In the movie *Tin Cup*—which is the consummate golfer movie, as it captures all of the golf jargon and many aspects of the game's ridiculousness—there is a line that resonates with me: "I guess you ride her until she bucks you." I appreciate this line because it reminds me that golf, just like life, has many ups and downs, twists and turns, peaks and valleys. When things are working, go with it until it stops working. Then what do you do? Reach out for feedback. Listen to, absorb, embrace, and appreciate what you receive with gratitude. Do your very best to apply the information. Redesign and reinvent yourself. We are uniquely qualified to alter our existence, to change our circumstances, to transform ourselves and create a life worth living. Sooner or later, you'll get hot again—you'll find your game, your stride, and the ultimate power zone. No one can clip your wings unless you let them. As Thomas Edison once said, "Many of life's failures are people who did not realize how close they were to success when they gave up." When you behave as a champion, quitting is no longer an option, ever. Spread your wings and fly. You are limitless, boundless, and infinitely capable.

Chapter Four

CREATING A VISION-DRIVEN LIFE

FIGURATIVELY SPEAKING, most people need bifocals in order to see their own vision. Through the years, many of their hopes and dreams have shrunk to the point of becoming microscopic or non-existent. When we started out as children, all we had was a vision. A vision of who we would be and what we would become. We envisioned what life would bring us, or how our life would unfold. We contemplated the meaning and purpose of life. To a child, dreaming isn't something that only occurs while sleeping. Children use their minds to visualize and imagine endless possibilities throughout the day.

Think of how many times your parents scolded you because you weren't paying attention or listening to them while they were talking to you. What were you doing? Dreaming. How many times did your teacher or your coach tell you to wake up, focus on the task at hand, and be present? What were you doing? Daydreaming. What does the term daydream mean? Most of us think of the word as having a negative connotation because when we were young, it was used as a criticism of our behavior. Daydreaming was made wrong in our minds. So what did we do? We stopped daydreaming, and ultimately, we stopped dreaming altogether. Why? Because the shame of daydreaming led us to distractions from what we were "supposed" to be doing. By interpreting that dreaming is bad and wrong, we actually helped develop our comfort zone and ego. A surefire way to destroy dreaming is by burying our heads and hearts behind the walls of our comfort zones. Einstein discovered the Theory of Relativity and the equation $E = MC^2$. This discovery led to new possibilities in science and in our understanding of time and space. Now I have an equation I would like to introduce to you. This equation could lead you to a life worth living.

In plain terms: Vision + Committed Action = Transformation. Now take out a piece of paper and a pen, and let's start to dream again. Let's begin by doing a closed-eye meditation. Find a quiet place where you can relax. It may also help if you put on some soft instrumental music. Begin by closing your eyes. Now, take a slow deep breath, and release it gently. Let go of the tension, and allow yourself to let go of your physical body. Quiet your mind. Continue taking slow deep breaths, gently letting the air go. Concentrate on your breathing, and allow yourself to release any stress and anxiety in your body. Try to shut out all distractions or disruptions. See yourself in a beautiful scene from nature. Transport yourself to this location and allow yourself to experience it. Use all of your senses to embrace the wondrous beauty and peaceful serenity of the place. When you have reached a relaxed state, I want you to visualize the life you want to live. The life you imagine yourself living now, and in the future. What experience are you looking for? What results do you want? Visualize yourself transforming from a person with your current attitudes and behaviors, into your true authentic self. Imagine experiencing the power, confidence, love, joy, passion, focus, connection, and freedom you've always wanted. See yourself showing up, in your family, with your friends, in your community, and in your business life, as the highest version of yourself. See the people around you responding to your new self, experiencing being in a relationship with you, and in a way that reflects your example. Imagine yourself not only today, but in the future, during a family reunion, a special occasion, or maybe it's simply a celebration of life party. Visualize yourself as the person you have always wanted to be—without hesitation, without fear, without restrictions, open-hearted, passionate, intimate, laughing, playful, alive, free, and showing up as the source of joy. Experience your experience. Take it all in, breathe in gently, and release with a smile. Now go farther into the future: one year from now, two years, five years, ten years, twenty years, all the way throughout your entire lifetime. Give yourself permission to dream and create. You have no limitations, internal or external. Now ask yourself, what is your purpose in life? Three times, repeat the question. Respond without judgment, without editing—there are no wrong answers. Allow yourself to verbalize and respond. Whatever you say is perfect. Now visualize yourself living the life you always imagined, at the highest level possible, and not only making a difference for yourself, but making a profound difference in other people's lives. Experience your experience. Take it all in. After a few moments, begin to bring your awareness and consciousness back to the present. Now take a slow deep breath, exhaling gently. Slowly come back and then open your eyes.

With your paper and pen, start writing down what you visualized in your future—everything you imagined during the meditation. Be specific with your experience, and simply let the words flow without editing. What is your purpose and your vision for your life? The journey you take to get there is just as important and valuable as the end result. Everything starts from where you are right now. You don't have to wait until you're finally living that life—you can begin creating it and enjoying it the moment you envision it. What experiences do you intend to create in your family relationships, and in your company with your co-workers, your employees, your executive team? What experience do you intend to create across all aspects of your life?

The key to living versus existing is having a powerful vision, a meaningful vision, a profound vision. Without vision, life becomes a series of to-do lists, a series of obligations and have-to's. We lose the juice. We lose the meaning behind the actions. Your vision gives you a sense of purpose. As a result, you understand why you do what you do. Whether it's in your professional life or your personal life, if you want to create a life worth living, your vision guides your decision-making and takes you in a purposeful direction. So ask yourself: What is your underlying motive in life? What is your reason for living? What difference will you make to distinguish yourself in the world?

The process of creating and generating our visions is similar to looking into the future and bringing that type of purposeful future into the present. In order to achieve this, we place bench-marks along the way—specific ways to measure the success and to make sure we are on track. This will allow us to build towards our vision. We acknowledge the successes and achieved goals that occur during the journey. Acknowledgment is important for our spirit, our energy. We need to re-energize and recharge regularly. By doing so, we'll be hungry to step out again into our lives and to continue taking the necessary risks. Also, when appropriate, we need to acknowledge our breakdowns—the moments when we lose integrity, the times we fall short of our promises, or break our word to ourselves or to others. By acknowledging these shortcomings, we can restore our confidence and essentially regain our power.

Your vision is reflected in everything you do. It's reflected in how you live, and ultimately, in what you have in the end. It's a combination of results and experience. Everybody wants to have an abundance of money. But if you don't feel worthy, confident, or secure without money, your mindset will prohibit you from making the healthy, responsible, and wise choices needed to move in the direction of money. A very small percentage of the population can play and win the lottery. Why would you leave your vision to chance? Why would you wait for the universe to provide you with the abundance you desire?

There are millions of hopeful and hopeless people out there who are waiting for some mystical power to provide for them. It's a sad reflection of our society knowing so many people live with low self-esteem, and in such a deep level of desperation. They are living a visionless life. Maybe your vision will be so powerful and transformational that it will bring you the abundance you want and also provide incredible opportunities for people who are struggling with survival, struggling to find their purpose and reclaim their power.

Think about how many people are now millionaires as a result of Mark Zuckerberg's vision when creating Facebook. These are people who may have otherwise had reasonable incomes, solid and steady jobs as programmers and analysts, but they are now enjoying wildly abundant finances because of the vision of another person. Maybe you will become the next Zuckerberg, someone who creates fantastic opportunities for other people.

Most people who are financially successful are driven by their vision, their purpose, and by their desire to have an abundance of money. The steps they take each day help move them towards their professional and personal goals. Their positive and optimistic attitudes attract infinite possibilities.

On the other hand, if you apply for a job at a time when you're desperately in need of one, that neediness will often rear its ugly head during the interview process. Employers don't want to hire people who are "in need." They want to hire people who are confident, powerful, and skillful—people who feel worthy and exude success. A positive outlook will reflect in what you do and how you do it. Employers want to hire people who are committed, who are hungry—but not desperate—to create extraordinary results. They are looking for people who are at ease and comfortable in their communication and it's often reflected in their body language. If you are coming from a place of need, the limiting voices of survival will become dominant, loud, and overpowering.

Take a moment to pause. *Let the fear pass.* Take a deep breath and reconnect with your inner mantra. If you resist fear and anxiety, other people will sense it. Embrace the fear, let it go, and then they will see and feel the calm demeanor emanating from you. It is possible for you to be hired "in need," for lesser money, for lesser opportunity. But you have now put yourself in the position of a victim—the employer is doing you a favor by hiring you. You have lost power and influence in the situation. Your lack of vision can create a lack of abundance financially, and it's important that you realize and recognize the breakdown isn't outside of you. You are not a victim of circumstance. Ultimately, you are the cause and source.

A marriage needs to occur between the vision, the purpose, the creation, and the daily/weekly/monthly benchmarks, successes, and celebrations along the way. If you have a vision and are committed to creating a life worth living, but the actions you've been taking are incongruent with that, you need to figure out how to fix it. Learn how to refocus and center yourself.

Life is not perfect. We are not perfect. We are human beings. We make mistakes. Life is a game of excellence, and excellence is possible. It is obtainable. It is achievable. But excellence is not perfection. If you go back to school, you can get an "A" with a grade of 90. A 90 is not perfect, but a 90 is an "A." You must leave room for error in your life. You must leave room for course correction and attitude adjustments. This involves having a healthy relationship with your intended and actual results. Be open to feedback, and have a healthy relationship with the feedback you receive from others. If you can use that feedback to improve and re-evaluate, you can get yourself back on track to accomplish what you set out to do. When you believe the issues blocking your success are due to circumstances beyond your control, you never have to accept responsibility for your actions. However, that kind of mindset still won't change the results or the outcome. It certainly will never support you in successfully creating your vision. Therefore, always remember these words: "I have met the enemy, and it is I." The only thing you can really control is yourself, and even though that's true, why would you want to control anyone or anything, anyway? Control is ego. It's restricting, tight, limiting. It's the opposite of power. Power creates, power expands, power is energy, power is a life force, power empowers, power is freedom. *Without power, vision is not possible.*

Many of you are perfectionists. Perfection is the equivalent of playing a game you can never win. The quest for perfection stems from an unrealistic vision of how life—or something more specific—is "supposed" to be. When you operate from the context of perfection, you are setting yourself up to fail right off the bat by attempting to achieve the unachievable. A vision is something we want to experience or achieve in the future. It should also be something that is truly possible and attainable. If you've ever been in a relationship with a perfectionist, you understand how important this is. Perfectionists can never take a compliment and are usually impossible to please. All they can see is what's missing, what's not working, what's wrong, and all the short-comings along the way. They constantly struggle with experiencing the joy of living due to the stress and pressure they put on themselves and their relationships. They are rarely present. Instead, they are relentlessly focused on their lack of accomplishment and their unfulfilled expectations. This, my friends, can be a total drag. It sucks all the energy from life. Imagine that your vision for a relationship is like a hot air balloon: full of passion, enthusiasm, excitement, and energy. You are ready to fly and soar, and then you realize the perfectionist is poking a hole in the fabric and the helium is slowly leaking out. Womp *womp*.

You might be wondering what the distinction is between a goal and a vision. Many people think they are the same thing, but there is a subtle difference. A goal is something specific and tangible, something that can be measured. Goals are often commitments to achieve—something based on an existing vision. It's the desire to achieve a higher level of results during the process. For example, someone might say, "I'm committed to losing a certain number of pounds this year. I'm committed to making a certain amount of money in 2015. I'm committed to generating a higher level of income, maybe 5%, 10%, or 25% more than I did the year before."

If someone is committed to a vision of improving their health, they set goals inside the vision. If you're an entrepreneur, the vision itself is for the creation of the company on a global scale, and to create the organizational environment to reflect that vision. Corresponding goals could be to develop a new product, a new product line, a new strategy to sell it, a revised plan to increase profitability, etc.

Declaring a vision is creating a future without precedent, a future without limitations, a statement of what's possible for you and for the world around you. Your vision can also be measured by results. For example, maybe you have a vision to start your own business, to have a family, to create peace, love, and harmony in the world, or to establish a healthy, honest, and authentic relationship. But sometimes, a vision is more focused on the way you are committed to experiencing your life and the world around you. It's more difficult to measure the intangible and abstract forms of vision because everyone interprets things differently. For example, I have a vision that guides all my personal and professional choices. My vision is to create peace, love, unity, and abundance for all. I filter my decisions on a micro and macro level through the prism of my vision. The vision itself is not tangible, but when I make choices, decisions, and take actions in my daily life, the vision becomes tangible through the declaration and manifestation of individual goals.

Visions are *adaptable* and *changeable*. They are not carved in stone. A vision can always be changed or adjusted. It can take a new direction. A vision can also expand and become more specific. Let's say your vision is to create peace and forgiveness in your family. Well, the implication is that some turmoil or breakdown has occurred in your relationships. Maybe your family has been separated. Maybe you're all living in different parts of the country and barely spend any quality time together. In the business of life, you've lost touch with the importance of your family. Everyone in the family misses the time you used to spend together and wants to reclaim it, but somebody needs to be the one to take a stand at some point. You need to step up and make a commitment to bring your family back together by declaring it as your vision. Then you must do what all visionaries do—empower, inspire, and enroll.

Your vision could evolve over time. You could start by talking on the phone together once a week. I'm talking about the core members—your parents, your brothers and sisters, your children, everyone you consider part of the family. Maybe you could make the commitment to host a family reunion once a year. From there, your vision could evolve into an annual family get-together at an exotic location. You might decide to attend therapy together, to participate in a transformational training that would allow you to break through the barriers or ineffective past experiences that have gotten in the way of creating what you desire in your lives. The vision to create peace, love, and forgiveness can take many different forms.

What happens when you accomplish creating peace, love, and forgiveness in your family? Does that mean your family stops evolving? Does it mean that you stop breaking new ground to bask in complacency? A vision can evolve to new levels, but a vision never loses its power because it comes from your purpose in life. It changes in form and structure, but not in spirit. In my experience, relationships—whether they're familial, professional, or personal—are constantly expanding or contracting. They're like plants that need to be watered on an ongoing basis. A fern won't grow in the desert by itself. It needs a nurturing environment. So if a relationship is not growing and expanding, if we don't explore new adventures and possibilities, or new ways of being, then the relationship becomes stagnant. It becomes dull. It loses its passion, and we wind up existing and surviving instead of living. During my years as a coach and trainer, I have encountered countless people who either have lost their vision or had no vision to begin with. Helen Keller once said, "The only thing worse than being blind is having sight, but no vision." What if you viewed your relationships as precious cargo that must be "handled with care" at all times? Imagine what you could create and experience as a result.

Professional relationships can be treated the same way. They also need nurturing if we want to continue growing and expanding. Everybody has talent. *Everybody.* However, not everybody's gifts are the same. Metaphorically, everybody wants to be the quarterback on the football team. Everybody wants to be the head cheerleader. Everybody wants to be Beyoncé, Bono, Steve Jobs, Bill Gates, or Oprah Winfrey. In other words, everybody wants to be extraordinary, talented, and rich. Deep down, everyone aspires to be the best, whether we are writers, directors, singers, leaders, business people, or teachers. But we're not all talented and gifted in the same way.

I have a friend who, for years and years and years, wanted to be a transformational trainer. His vision was to make a difference in people's lives by coaching them to discover their possibilities and magnificence. One of his lifelong passions and talents is writing. Over the years, he has written everything from poetry to screenplays.

When I need assistance with creating writing materials, documents, and handouts for my workshops, he has always been at the top of my list of people to reach out to. Why? Because I'm familiar with his writing abilities and believe he is more than competent in this area. For sure, he is much more competent than I am. Writing has never been my area of expertise. My talents and skills are in the domain of public speaking, coaching, and focusing on vision creation—the theory and ideas behind something. I'm a creator. I'm an entrepreneur. I see the big picture. I see the possibilities. I don't always see the details needed to put it together.

One day, this friend and I had an honest, direct, and uncomfortable meeting. I sat down with him and said, "I think you're amazing, you're talented, you're gifted, and here's why." I listed off everything I admired, respected, and appreciated about him. It was important to acknowledge these special qualities to support him in opening up, so that he would understand that I genuinely care about him. This made it easier for him to hear the difficult feedback. I said, "You can go to the *Hall of Fame of Life*. You can make lots of money and be extremely successful in any area related to technology or writing. You could be a screenwriter or a poet. I believe you have the talent to make it big. What I'm about to say—even though it might be hard to hear—comes from the bottom of my heart, because I care enough about you to be honest." I went on to say, "You will never be a trainer. You just don't have what it takes."

He'd given me full permission to speak openly and honestly, as he was the one seeking the feedback. Immediately, he was disappointed, devastated, and crushed by my assessment. Obviously, it wasn't what he hoped to hear. However, he trusted me to tell him what I truly saw was possible or not possible. Of course, it was emotionally difficult for me as well. He's been a great friend of mine for many years, and the last thing I wanted to do was hurt him. But if I lied or told him only what he wanted to hear, would it help him get where he wanted to be? Absolutely not. I knew my opinion would be difficult for him to hear because he was living in an illusion created by his ego and not based on any legitimate evidence. I didn't want to say it, but in the end I had to tell the honest truth. I have been a coach and trainer for thirty years. I'm not a politician who is running for office and will make "promises" to people in exchange for a vote. One of the most important aspects of coaching is to tell the truth about what I see is working or not working, regardless of the discomfort it might cause either party. Always remember this old adage: "The truth will set you free."

I'm not just excellent at what I do and the way I do it. I know a lot of other people who are excellent in different versions of what I do. Some people have it and some people don't. In Hollywood, they call this the "It Factor." Well, the same phenomenon can be found in coaching and training, too. At the end of the day, someone in my field of work must have a certain *je ne sais quoi*, a touch of magic. It's not the words we use, but the music behind those words. In other words, it's not what you say, but how you say it. It's an innate ability to become transparent and shape-shift to connect with a wide range of clients and students with different needs and wants. To be able to do it naturally and authentically is the difference between the masters and the pretenders.

Some people have the potential but not the rigor and work ethic required to achieve it. And still others want it, but just don't have it. Friends and family really need to learn how to care enough about each other to be honest. All I wanted was for my friend to discover a vision and purpose that would allow him to become a success and create extraordinary results. I wanted him to find a platform for his natural talents, gifts, and skills, so that he could shine. He happens to be one of the most intelligent, conscious, and evolved people I've ever known. I have a tremendous amount of respect for him. Some of you might feel that my comment was a personal attack against him. Absolutely not. It was honest feedback for a good friend. To this day, I stand by what I said. Here we are, ten years later, and he is finally starting to structure and design a vehicle for his career where he can manifest his vision and create a life worth living. And he's doing it! Maybe he didn't have the tools necessary to do the work I do, the way I do it, but he found his path and is making his way. He started his own business and provides consulting services to a wide range of companies. He also went back to college to get his master's degree. He's done things with his life that I can only dream of. I'm so proud of him.

Everybody has talents and gifts. Everybody has unique abilities. The opportunity for you is to discover and be conscious of what they are. If you're unsure, reach out to get a wide variety of feedback and input. Don't just go to your family members or friends. Imagine the distinctive information you will receive if you were to approach people in relationships that are not working or relationships where you experienced some kind of conflict, in the past or present. These people could include ex-lovers and ex-spouses, former bosses, competitors, and maybe even someone who you know doesn't like you. Feedback from them could be very helpful, or at the very least, humbling. If you have a loving and connected relationship with your mother, it's possible she will just tell you what you want to hear, so take her comments with a grain of salt. If you go to your exes, they might tell you what you don't want to hear. In other words, they might not be able to see any of your positive qualities. Instead, they might spend all their time talking about your faults, everything that's missing from your life, everything you do wrong, and so on. See if you can sift through the pain of that feedback to find those possibly hidden gems, even if they are buried among negative comments. In some relationships, objectivity is a challenge. In the process of learning and discovering your strengths and talents, you would be creating the opportunity for people to contribute to you, some who may have stopped caring because of what you did or didn't do in the past. The result could also be a healing and forgiving process.

Now, organize and compile all the information you received. Take it all in, absorb it. Go on the internet and research different careers, job opportunities, and businesses. Take a look at and really consider the diverse types of work that are available and genuinely possible for you, and narrow it down from there. Another tool that could be useful is a personality assessment test, like the Myers-Briggs. You can even take an aptitude test. Don't worry about it being called a "test." There are no right or wrong answers here. Just respond honestly and stay true to who you are. Based on your answers to the questions, you will then receive a list of potential jobs and careers that could be a good fit for you. If anything, it's a solid place to start.

Remember, a career is not a vision. A career is a vehicle for you to create opportunities to use your skills, intelligence, personality strengths, and talents, in order to benefit a business or organization, and to receive financial compensation and growth opportunities. Your career exists inside of your vision.

Maybe you want to be a stockbroker because you have the desire and passion to make a lot of money, but maybe their reputation of questionable integrity doesn't sit well with you. Of course, not all stockbrokers lack integrity, but they are in a business where sometimes it seems they will do almost anything to get a sale, due to the high-pressure environment and the stiff competition. In order to maintain your integrity, you might have to settle for $1,000,000 a year, instead of $2,000,000. Would it be worth it?

As long as you make a living and earn your money legally, it's up to you to decide what your vision and values are, and to follow the path of consistency. No matter which career you choose, which business path you choose in order to create a life worth living, make sure it's something that allows your skills, talents, and gifts to thrive—not just survive, but thrive. Remember, creating results is amazing and something we all want, but it's also how we create the results that matters most and makes all of the difference in the end.

We're all going to die eventually. There is no way out of that certainty. That is an option we do not have. What matters is what you do, what you create, and what you cause in your life and in the world before you go. Eventually we disappear, and some of us will disappear even before we actually pass away. Is the latter scenario really what you want? The career you choose could be the difference between not only living and surviving, but also how long you actually live. You have a much better opportunity to create the quality of life you want, and the longevity of living to see the fruits of your labor, if you find a vehicle you can excel at. This way, no matter what level you start at, there's another level waiting once you've achieved mastery of that first level. Then there's a third level, and then a fourth. There are never-ending opportunities for your economic growth. Would that support you in creating a life worth living? As Steve Jobs so eloquently stated, "Your work is going to be a large part of your life, and the only way to be truly satisfied is to do what you believe is great work. And the only way to do great work is to love what you do. If you haven't found it yet, keep looking. Don't settle. As with all matters of the heart, you'll know when you find it."

Speaking of Apple's co-founder, let's take a look at his company. One of the many things I admire about the Apple organization is the people who work in their stores. They literally love their jobs. When I say love, I mean *love*. Now, why do they love working at Apple? In part, I'm sure it's because they are avid fans and consumers of the products. But Apple also opens the door for a wide range of employees with very unique backgrounds and cultures. They actually value diversity during the hiring process; they are not interested in society's view of what's "normal." The Apple family is a fantastic example of a melting pot. Walk into any Apple store and check out the people who work there. I promise, very few companies in the world can boast such a wide variety of eclectic personality types.

My son Nick is one of their employees. On his very first day of work at Apple, the manager started by showing Nick around the store. They walked through the different aisles and looked at the vast array of products, from iPhones to MacBook Pro computers. Nick was getting the whole tour before the store opened for the morning, and then his manager said, "Hey, let's go and check out the back office." When he opened the door to the employee lounge, all the employees who worked for this particular Apple store were waiting in the back. Nick walked in, and everybody suddenly started chanting his name in unison: "Nick, Nick, Nick, Nick, Nick!" They went crazy chanting his name over and over again. My son was in complete shock. This was definitely not what he expected on his first day. It was like they had thrown a special surprise party for Nick. After the chant, they jumped on him and started hugging him, giving him high-fives, and welcoming him to the team. This is an entry-level retail job we're talking about. Who wouldn't love working for Apple if this is what it's like? Everybody loves working for Apple. There are opportunities at all levels, starting with the entry-level retail position. Then they go from retail sales, to Expert, to Genius, to Business Manager, etc. Of course, there are also opportunities all the way up to Apple Corporate in Cupertino, California. What a perfect vehicle to manifest your business vision in an environment of never-ending opportunities, both for the organization and for the employees.

Imagine if every business was like Apple. It doesn't matter if you work at a Denny's or if you work for AT&T. It doesn't matter if you work for American Airlines. It doesn't matter if you're the janitor at the Dallas Cowboys football stadium. In every environment, in all jobs or careers, you have an opportunity to enhance your experience and opportunity for growth. Martin Luther King, Jr. once said, "Don't just set out to do a good job. Set out to do such a good job that the living, the dead, and the unborn couldn't do it any better." If you showed up to work this way, what opportunities would you create?

Several years ago, when the world of technology was just beginning to explode with the introduction of the internet, Apple was growing and expanding at such a rapid rate that it couldn't keep up with the demand of the Macintosh computer. Recent college graduates were getting life-changing opportunities to work for companies like Apple, Microsoft, HP, and Dell, but also creating opportunities to go into business for themselves. Steve Jobs and Bill Gates both attended college, but neither finished. In our society today, we call them "college dropouts." In my generation, we had a different term to describe people who dropped out of college: "LOSERS." But now we have another word to describe these two men: VISIONARIES. The fact that these two men could become two of the most successful and influential business people in the history of the world, created a complete paradigm shift in our culture. We had always heard, since childhood, that the only way we could ever be successful was by obtaining a college degree. It was an idea perpetuated by our parents, teachers, advisors, peers, advertising, TV, and the media. But then, these two geniuses came along and completely altered our socially accepted viewpoint. In doing so, they opened up a whole new interpretation of what it requires to be successful, and what it takes not only to have a vision, but to be a visionary.

During this time of change, Apple was forced to think fast, on the fly. They were on the cutting edge of technology, but they also needed to be on the cutting edge of creating an infrastructure to support the extraordinary growth in sales. They created an advertising campaign to attract new employees from the top graduates at the best schools in America. The ad proclaimed, about the company: "Not only ahead of its time as a business and entrepreneur, but ahead of its time in hiring quality contributors." Jobs was smart enough to know that if he could do what he did, there would be others who would follow his lead and take his quest to heights and levels that not even he could envision.. He knew that it was only a matter of time before the next big cutting-edge company—such as Google, Facebook, Yahoo!, and more—would materialize. Instead of fighting against the grain, Apple decided they were going to adapt and adjust to this new environment, this new culture, this new climate. They decided to bring in potential employees by giving them an incredible opportunity for five years. They realized upfront that in five years, these young talents would probably move on to something new. Apple surrendered to the explosion of technology and computer science that they helped perpetuate. Technology is constantly evolving.

Even NASA was in danger of going out of business recently, but now NASA's thriving again—creating new opportunities for science, engineering, space exploration, and of course, technology. There are infinite possibilities available for people in every field. You get to create your own business and become an entrepreneur or find a company that fits your skills. That gives you the opportunity to grow exponentially with no limits. You could even become an entrepreneur and create your own business vision inside someone else's organization. You owe it to yourself to manifest your vision in its highest form. Think about what Bob Marley meant when he said, "Emancipate yourselves from mental slavery, none but ourselves can free our minds!" If you free your mind and open your eyes, if you look into the future without blinders on, what do you see?

You need to find a game or a vehicle that fits your personality and toolset and is in alignment with creating a life worth living. You are not rich by virtue of having a billion dollars. You could be a schoolteacher, make $30,000 a year, and be rich. Rich with the knowledge that you're making a difference in those children's lives. Full in your experience of life through developing the future leaders in our society. You're educating not just any children, but *our* children. You're empowering them and motivating them. You have a chance to be a role model and set an example, so that today's children realize how much they matter, not only to themselves, but also to their family, to society, and to the world. You could be the single most influential person in a child's life. The result could be that they become the doctor who discovers a cure for cancer or AIDS. Maybe your inspiration and belief in them taught them how to study and to care about studying, or maybe you challenged them to think and to push beyond the boundaries of limited thinking. Maybe you invited them to be creative and to express their original ideas, or maybe you showed them you care and instilled in them the confidence they needed but weren't getting at home. Now that, my friends, is a rich and vision-driven life.

When your life is rich, it doesn't matter how much money you make. You wouldn't give up what you have for anything. It's a life worth living and you're living it. On the other hand, you could be a billionaire who is lonely, fear-driven, scarcity-driven, selfish, and self-centered. At the end of the day, all you'd have is your money. Yes, maybe you'd have a trophy wife or the "right" husband waiting at home. Maybe you'd have kids who go to an expensive private school. Maybe you'd have vintage cars and mansions and all the objects that our society says we should desire, but you'd feel desperate and alone, whether in public or in private. Just because you have money does not mean that you're creating a life worth living. What if you changed your relationship with money? What if you saw money as a tool for you to use? What if how much you have or make isn't who you are? How could this new interpretation change your life and your experience of living? Your life experience isn't determined by what you have or don't have. It's determined by the experiences you create from moment to moment.

I want to present you with four powerful, influential, and inspiring leaders who had every reason in the world to become nobodies, to play the victim card and spend their days as mediocre survivalists who never made a significant impact in their lives or the lives of others. Steve Jobs, Sir Richard Branson, Oprah, and Ellen DeGeneres are all excellent examples of people who have created something out of nothing, made vision-driven lives for themselves. They each come from vastly different backgrounds and took their own paths in order to reach success. Their journeys have defied the odds, and their success was not delivered to them on a silver platter. They had anything but a head start. The path to success wasn't paved for them by anyone else. Each individual is an entrepreneur who created something extraordinary. Each is a visionary who decided, to quote from the TV series *Star Trek*, "to boldly go where no man has gone before."

Steve Jobs was given up for adoption at birth. His own parents, for whatever reason, were not prepared or willing to raise him. He had the perfect excuse to play the victim, to think, "If my own parents didn't want me and gave me up, why would I matter to anyone else? Something must be wrong with me. I'm nobody special." But Steve Jobs was adopted by parents who clearly loved him and were devoted to him. They loved him, accepted him, and not only provided for his education, but also inspired him to believe in his value and his passions. By choosing to adopt him and by treating him as if he were their own, they gave him an opportunity to do something with his life.

After attending one year of college, Jobs and his friend Steve Wozniak had a vision, an idea for a new business, an innovative product. They called it Apple. They turned his parents' garage into a working laboratory. Let's take a moment to dissect this situation. An orphan college dropout is hanging out with his buddy, smoking pot in his garage, and working day and night on this new project. They ended up launching Apple straight from that garage. During the early years, Apple enjoyed some success with the Macintosh computer. That is, until the board of directors, which Jobs himself hired, fired him from his position as the CEO. The company that *he* created, the company that *he* started in his garage, fired him. When has anything like that ever happened before? Imagine creating your own company, building it from the ground up, and hiring a board of directors, only for them to vote you out. So, Jobs left.

When he left, he didn't quit, give up, feel sorry for himself, or bury his head in the sand. Jobs went on to create two new companies, Next and Pixar, and additionally became a significant stockholder of Disney. Certainly, everyone remembers the movie *Toy Story*, the first of many hit films created by Pixar. Jobs was vision-driven, not Apple-driven. That mindset clearly allowed him to connect with visions and possibilities other people weren't able to see. This extraordinary ability to connect with his own vision opened up his ability to surround himself with like-minded leaders with their own unique gifts, and as a result, he was able to create multiple successful businesses, not just one.

While Jobs was enjoying his extraordinary successes elsewhere, the Apple business and its profits started going down, and its value on the stock market plummeted with it. The Apple Board of Directors called Steve Jobs up, asked him to come back in, and they ultimately rehired him for the position of CEO. Not only that, but they bought out his company, Next, for a mere $427 million dollars. This was a company he had started with $7 million.

Upon returning, Jobs built Apple into the most successful business in the entire world. If Apple were a country unto itself, it is estimated to be in the top 100 wealthiest countries with over 170 billion dollars in cash. Just imagine that. Apple products are innovative, cutting-edge, useful, and valuable. Your children can use them as educational tools, you can use them in high school and in college for homework and projects, and you can use them in all facets of business. Apple's products reach out and touch all aspects of personal and professional life, from pleasure to work.

Jobs developed this incredible company and surrounded himself with an amazing championship team. When he got sick with cancer and eventually passed away a few years ago, he was able to pass the baton to the next generation of leadership. He turned the company over to another incredible and courageous visionary, Tim Cook, who has now taken Apple to a whole new level of possibility and success.

Next, we have Sir Richard Branson, who is the owner and founder of Virgin Records. Branson dropped out of high school. He didn't drop out of college like Steven Jobs; he never went to college at all. When he was sixteen years old, he became a rock-and-roll journalist. He wrote reviews and critiques of artists and their new albums. His passion was music and being involved in the music business. Over time, he developed credibility in the industry through his writing. Ironically, as a child he had been diagnosed with dyslexia, but he never let it stop him from becoming an excellent and well-respected writer. However, like so many of us, he wanted to be directly involved in making music, not just reporting on it. He found the courage to declare his vision and make it a reality. At twenty-two years old, Richard Branson created Virgin Records. He went from being a journalist, writing about what others create, to being an entrepreneur who was authoring his own path. Virgin Records became one of the largest and most successful music companies in the world.

But of course, being a visionary, Branson still wasn't satisfied. He went to the next level and decided to venture into the airline business. From there, he developed Virgin Atlantic and Virgin Airlines. If you've ever been on a Virgin Atlantic or Virgin Airlines flight, you know that it's a completely unique experience, from the cabin lighting to the flight procedures. Branson also has a brilliant sense of humor, as evidenced when he said, "The best way for a billionaire to become a millionaire is to buy an airline." The fact that he can have a sense of humor about a topic that people often take too seriously is inspirational.

One of the ways he has revolutionized the flying experience is through the announcements of emergency procedures. Normally, no one listens to these. Everyone is immediately disconnected, talking on the phone, or typing out one last email before the plane takes off. I feel like I've heard this justification a thousand times: "If the plane is going down, it's not going to make any difference anyway." But Branson is a visionary and an entrepreneur.

He thought to himself, "What can we do to get people's attention?" He dug deep into his vast expertise and actually developed a music video. Now, when the video is playing, complete with singing and dancing, all the passengers are watching the screen and paying close attention to the emergency procedures. Not to mention the fact that the music is catchy, so the passengers find themselves humming along and tapping their feet to the beat. It may not make a difference if the plane crashes, but I can promise that it creates a different vibe on the plane. Everyone is present and attentive.

Through his vision, Sir Richard Branson brought the Virgin Records and music industry experience into his airplane business. And still, that wasn't enough for him. Now he's taking his vision to the next level of outrageousness by creating Virgin Galactic, which is a plane that will take passengers into space, just for fun. Many of us dreamed of being astronauts or traveling to space when we were younger, but didn't pursue the opportunity. Lots of people love to live on the edge through participation in extreme sports, like bungee jumping from tall bridges in New Zealand. Branson's vision has created the perfect opportunity for thrill-seekers, and of course, for people who like to go super fast and want to touch the sky. Clearly, this adventure would be for people who are looking for the ultimate, once-in-a-lifetime experience. Years ago, when I was a child, I remember watching movies and reading comic books that detailed random space travel. As someone who was afraid of heights and experienced horrible motion sickness, I had no desire to be an astronaut, but I was always fascinated by outer space and the question of what might be out there. I would imagine life in the future, and how space travel would be part of our everyday existence. My friends and I were convinced that there was life on other planets, and we wanted to see it for ourselves someday.

Well, Sir Richard Branson is now making it possible for anyone who can afford it to travel to space. Not only is it an outrageous vision, but it's quite possibly another profitable venture for Branson. His ability to communicate and translate his unique vision is so successful that he's already had over four hundred people pay $200,000 per seat for the flight. Imagine getting those numbers, those results! Sir Richard Branson is a visionary who is creating a life worth living, not only for himself but also for many other people. This is the same man who dropped out of high school and never went to college, never had a formal education.

I saw Richard Branson speak a few years ago at the Ernst & Young Entrepreneur of the Year Convention in Palm Springs, California. The thing I admired most about him was his charismatic, passionate, and inspiring personality. He was smiling during the entire presentation. He smiles like he's happy for no reason. I'm sure he enjoys being a billionaire, being involved in a multitude of different businesses and creative projects, and receiving acknowledgement and recognition for his accomplishments in life. However, I believe the source of his smile comes from his belief in himself and the power that he has to choose. The result is that Richard Branson exudes happiness to everyone, everywhere. It must be working because I find myself smiling while I write this segment of the book.

His newest vision is to wipe out the concept of vacation days so that people are no longer "earning" vacations, and he's leading by example within his own companies. His idea is that everyone can take as much vacation time as they want, as long as they do their jobs. All you have to do is keep up with your work, and you can be on vacation for two weeks, for two months, every other week, you can work only four days per week—it's completely up to you. Come in when you want, leave when you want, just do your job. If you can do your job in less than 40 hours a week, do it in less than 40 hours a week. Some business people would call this insane. They would be terrified that employees might manipulate the opportunity, not get their work done, and of course, the company would suffer as a result.

This is revolutionary. It's transformational, outrageous, and a radical risk. It's the epitome of living on the Skinny Branches of the tree of life. People who think like this are willing to declare it publicly regardless of the scrutiny, regardless of the ridicule. Some businesses seem not to care about human resources, or about the quality of life for their employees. Often, it seems like they only care about their money, the results, the performance, and the profit of the company. People like Sir Richard Branson are always thinking beyond that. And quite frankly, he doesn't care what the popular business theorists say. Why should he? He has defied all conventional wisdom regarding "the right way" to pursue business success since the day he started, by dropping out of high school. In doing so, he may have dropped out of society's interpretation of the usual path to success, but he dropped into his VISION instead. His vision is clearly the captain of the aircraft called his life.

How about Oprah Winfrey? Oprah has her own television channel. Forget about having one of the most successful talk shows in the history of television. She owns OWN. It sounds insane. Nobody has his or her own television channel. But Oprah does.

Oprah is an African American woman. She was abused as a child, and experienced poverty, racism, and segregation while living in the South in the 1960s. She was bullied and treated like a second-class citizen. Oprah was raised by a single mother and even got pregnant at fourteen but lost the baby, who died as an infant. She had every excuse in the world to play the victim, to hide from the world, to think that she wasn't worth anything, and to go through her life just surviving and existing. Instead, she chose to rise up, to not let anyone clip her wings, and she has turned out to be the most successful, influential, and wealthy female entertainer in the world.

She's worth more and has accomplished more than most everyone in the world, but on top of that, she is an inspiration and a role model. A true visionary. Oprah contributes to society in many ways, whether it's by opening up schools in Africa, supporting women who are victims of domestic violence, taking a stand to end racism and bring our vast American cultures together, or by taking action through countless charitable activities. This is a woman who uses her power to influence and empower others. Oprah uses her power to make a difference, to create opportunities for people who might not have them otherwise. She is creating a life worth living and has directly impacted women, minorities, and entire nations around the globe. She's working to interconnect the United States with other parts of the world, bringing everyone closer together. Because of her, we have opportunities to work together to make a difference so that everybody wins. Oprah's vision expands across not only the United States, but throughout the world. Against all odds, she's leading the way for us all.

Ellen DeGeneres is another excellent example of vision-driven leadership. What I admire about Ellen is that she essentially created a new career, a new vision, for herself. She understands the idea of redesign and reinvention. Honesty and authenticity can sometimes create, in uncanny ways, a new level of freedom and choice that most people don't even know exist. Ellen started out as a comedian, and of course, she was very funny and enjoyed gradual success. She started in clubs and worked her way up to the series *Here and Now*, her own stand-up special on HBO. During this time, she chose to keep her sexuality a secret and out of the press. What would society do if they found out she was gay? Would they accept her? Would they judge and reject her? Would she lose her career?

One day, she found the courage to acknowledge her sexuality and came out to the general public. The reaction was basically no reaction at all. When she had the confidence to be honest about who she is, she gave people the opportunity to be authentic with themselves. She was a risk-taker, and even if that wasn't her original intention when she decided to come out, it empowered many others to do the same. Her own popularity did not diminish; it actually increased. She created multiple opportunities for herself, including hosting some of the biggest events in the world of entertainment, the Oscars and the Grammys. In fact, she became so successful and popular as a stand-up comic, that she was given her own national TV show. Currently, she hosts one of the most successful talk shows in the United States and has won a whopping thirteen Emmy Awards. Wow, that's impressive! Here is an openly gay woman with a talk show in the United States, who pushes buttons and challenges her guests with her witty but frank interviewing style. She doesn't avoid tough issues or challenging topics. She doesn't avoid the discomfort of putting herself at risk. She's on the Skinny Branches of the tree. She lives with passion, joy, and love. She brings her wife Portia onto the show constantly. We see them together, and they're not hiding their life from the world. They're out, literally out. They're role models, courageously living authentically, both for themselves and as an example for other people.

One of my favorite parts of Ellen's show is how she begins by dancing. She dances every day and doesn't care how she dances, or whether she does it "right," or how it makes her look. It may seem like a small thing, but it brings people joy. If you're in the audience, you get up on your feet and boogie right along with her. When I watch her show, I see her moving with passion through the audience while the music is pumping. She is an inspiration, a leader, and a role model. She makes a difference for so many people, and she is such a wonderful example of creating a life worth living. Ellen's vision is unfolding and I can't wait to see and experience the next level of evolution.

Many of us are so busy that we never make time for fun: to dance, to sing, to laugh, to play, to get dirty on the playground, to participate in extracurricular activities. It's just work, work, work, all the time. Every day is full of endless activities and busyness. What do you want to create in your everyday living experience? It can be created from the bottom up, not just from the top down. For those of you who are business owners, it's your responsibility not only to lead the business, but also to create the environment that you desire for your business and for the people who work in it. For those who aren't business owners yet, you can help create the kind of environment you would want to work in with your teammates. What about at home with your family? What do you want to create daily in that space?

A vision begins with the question, "What do you want?" On the surface level, everybody has something he or she wants. This is the tip of the iceberg. You might say, "I want to make money. I want a BMW or a Rolex. I want to travel. I want to be thinner." But if you peel away the surface layers and dig deeper into what you *really* want, you've reached the beginning stages of what I'm talking about. Ask yourself what you want in your life. What do you want people to say about you when they're asked? When people hear your name, what are the qualities you want them to think of? You can't stop people from having a certain opinion of you, but you can affect their thoughts and experiences by living your vision and using your inner mantra.

Here is a step-by-step process to formulating your own vision.

Step 1: Imagine yourself in the future—one, two, five, ten, twenty years out, both personally and professionally. What is the life of your dreams? You have no limitations. Write it down and describe it in detail.

Step 2: What are the emotional experiences you want to be associated with the life of your dreams? For example, do you wish for love, connectivity, passion, intimacy, fun, adventure, freedom, joy, energy, fulfillment, satisfaction? Something else? It's your choice. Anything you desire is on the menu. You can also distinguish between your personal and professional lives.

Step 3: What are the values, attitudes, behaviors, and actions that will support you in manifesting this dream into reality? Be specific. Declare at least five.

Step 4: What are the first action steps you must take today, tomorrow, this week, this month, in order to bridge the gap between where you are now and the manifestation of the vision in your future? Before you land on the moon, let's get the rocket into space. Before we get it into space, let's get it off the launch pad. Work backwards. You see where to go from here.

Step 5: Commit to creating the vision. Give your word to yourself. It begins with you. You must be able to look in the mirror and honestly say, with courage, power, and authenticity, "I declare my vision. I will make it happen because I said so. I am the author of my life. I am the captain of my ship." Ask yourself, "What would Bill Gates do? What would Tim Cook do? What would Oprah do?" Now declare your vision to your world. Go big; hold nothing back. Be vulnerable. Share it with the people in your life who will hold you accountable.

Share your vision with passion. Visionaries are shameless. They don't care what people think. They don't care how they look. They don't care if it's right or wrong. They're open to scrutiny. They're vulnerable. They live on the Skinny Branches of the tree. Everybody's got a point of view. No leader, no creator, no author, no inventor, and no entrepreneur has ever existed without vulnerability, without a public declaration of his or her vision, and the scrutiny and criticism that comes with being bold. But visionaries are able to withstand the negativity because of their commitment to their vision. It embodies who they are, and they are embodied in it.

About thirty years ago, I declared my vision, which was to create peace, love, unity, and abundance in every aspect of my life. If I'm committed to creating peace, do I judge people? No. If I'm committed to creating love, do I withhold feelings of anger or frustration? No. I communicate whatever I need to in order to clear my pain, anger, or emotions. Then I let go of any frustration. Clean space, new moment. From there, I communicate pure thoughts based on possibilities. People will experience that I truly love and care about them by what I say and by what I do. I am committed to living my vision 24/7/365, with rigor. When I go on vacation, I take my vision with me. I never take a vacation from what matters to me. My behaviors, actions, and values are consistent with my vision.

The time to live out loud is now. We've all heard the expression, "Dance like nobody's watching." That's an attitude based on vision and living on the Skinny Branches of the tree. Apply it to your own life. You have to believe in your own vision. If you can't convince yourself of this vision, then no one else is going to get it either. You can't create your vision for anybody else. You can't do it to please anybody else. It has to be for you. It has to be authentic and genuine. When it's genuine and heartfelt, you can declare it out loud. Once you do, you're at stake. When a human being is at stake, when they're vulnerable and shamelessly committed, when we don't care how we look, when we don't care what other people think, don't care whether people approve or disapprove, or whether something is right or wrong—that's POWER! When you're in this state, you can create anything. You can create anything for yourself and for other people. When you live this way, you are attractive. You are a mover and shaker.

People like this inspire leadership in other people. They create a fire within other people. Yes, there will be criticism thrown their way. There will be risk. They continuously put themselves at stake. Some people die in the process of standing up for their vision and seeing it through. Often, their vision is so powerful that they are able to enroll others to carry it on, even after they're gone. When Martin Luther King died, his dream and vision lived on. When Gandhi died, his vision lived on, too. It doesn't just begin and end with you. You're the nucleus, and you're making an impact on everybody around you. The whole world benefits when a leader or a visionary is living on the Skinny Branches.

When I think of the term "vision-driven," I think of somebody who has clear intention behind what they do. How about creating a footprint in the world? Everybody will be remembered for something. People are going to talk about you, whether you want them to or not. Go back and remember that smile on Richard Branson's face. Yes, what he was talking about was amazing, but it was his smile and energy that left the biggest impact on everyone in the audience.

As human beings, parents, people, citizens, leaders, and business owners, our first step is to connect with our vision. Our vision is not a mission. A mission is what your company does. A vision is why you do what you do. What is your life's purpose? When you get out of bed in the morning, what is the vision that drives you? Live by your inner mantra. Use the mantra to interrupt the fear and self-doubt, to quiet your mind. Use it to center yourself. From the foundation of those words, declare and create your vision for your life. Then the words have power and life. They can ultimately become a filter for the way you live, and for the moment-to-moment choices you make as you move passionately and confidently towards the manifestation of your vision. As the Greek philosopher Plato once said, "Man is a being in search of meaning." Let the quest begin!

Chapter Five

LOVE THE JOURNEY

O FTEN, THERE IS A GAP between where we are currently, and the point where we are manifesting our vision. Many people tend to be spoiled, demanding, and controlling. They want what they want, when they want it. As human beings, we display a tremendous amount of impatience. We also experience intense frustration and resistance when we realize we aren't "there" yet. But what if there is nothing there at the finish line? What if it's not the satisfying result you were looking for? What if your arrival at the destination is actually the booby prize?

By nature, children often live in a fantasy world. In their heads, they will imagine a world far, far away. In some cases, this world is as far away as possible from their family or from the unappealing situation they're currently in. As human beings, one of our greatest challenges is to be present, to be fully engaged and connected with where we are, what we are doing, what we are feeling, and who we are with. Think about everything you miss because you're not present—those special moments that you can never get back. With loved ones. With children. Your son's first step, your daughter's first recital, your first date, your favorite team winning the big game. Instead of living in that moment, your mind is wondering, thinking about work, worrying about your to-do list, about something that's bothering you. Maybe your mind is on your fears or insecurities, or maybe you are simply thinking about nothing. Whenever you are not present, you are missing the wonders of life and all it has to offer.

Life occurs in the moment, in the journey. We have the opportunity to create the magic of living and develop a profound and deep appreciation for what it means to be alive. What if we viewed life, and the way we live it, as an honor and a privilege? What if, "Time is a precious thing," wasn't just a slogan to throw around? What if you decided not to take one more minute for granted? How would it change the way you live and the choices you make?

Some of us have a hard time even appreciating joy and love. We invalidate and minimize the feelings because we're so uncomfortable with them. We believe, on a certain level, that we don't deserve to feel that way. That we're not worthy of it. Life, as you know, is a long and winding road. Real living requires a healthy relationship with change. It will include risks, setbacks, failures, and sweet successes. Sometimes you will feel pride. Other times, you will feel incapable and overwhelmed. These conflicting feelings and thoughts can actually occur in the same day. But you must understand that a life worth living doesn't begin at some distant point in time. It starts now, with the first step, and then continues with the next, and then the next. You have the power to create the experiences you want to enjoy along the way. Use them as stepping stones within the bigger picture. You don't have to start at point A and suffer until you reach point Z. The journey from points B to Y is what makes the difference in the manifestation of your vision. This is where you shape and mold your life. You have the power and the ability to create your experiences in any way you wish. Whether you're crawling or climbing out onto the Skinny Branches, the process itself has to be rewarding, or you'll quickly lose the desire to go further.

You have to learn to love the process. You can't just love the results. If you only love the beginning and the end, you'll be in trouble after the first couple of steps. Your ability to travel through the in-between will determine whether you succeed or fail. Having a great idea is easy. Think of all the ideas you've ever had that you never brought to life. You know, sometimes you're sitting on the couch with your wife or your husband when you suddenly get what seems like a brilliant idea. And you're fired up now, but then you don't take any action to make it happen. Maybe you get caught up in your day-to-day life or your current responsibilities, and your brilliant idea never sees the light of day.

Life is a journey, not an event. Most people are in survival-mode—instead of living on the Skinny Branches, we're just going from event to event to event. We're activity-driven. The term "human being" is not really in line with how we are behaving in life. I think most people could more accurately be described as "human doings."

We've become activity junkies. We go from one activity to the next, but we're disconnected from life. Technology has revolutionized living and transformed the way we live in so many positive ways. Unfortunately, it has also had a negative impact because now we're even more disconnected than ever. Technology only makes being present even more difficult because it gives you a way to connect with everyone except for the people you are actually with. Why? Because you're not really *with* them. You're in their "neighborhood." We're disconnected in our relationships and in the way we communicate with people. We text

"I love you" instead of saying it in person. Many people no longer bother calling to experience live communication. We're too lazy and "busy," and we don't even make time to spell out words in full. We've turned our love, among other things, into acronyms: ILY, BFF, TTYL.

This is what I refer to as drive-by love. It's drive-by communication. It's not authentic. It's not meaningful. It's not rich. Part of the journey of life is enhancing the little moments, not speeding right past them. When we were children and saw a bird fly above our heads or an airplane in the sky, we would stop in our tracks with awe and wonder. We asked millions of questions, wondered "why" the world was the way it was: "Why is the sky blue? Why am I a boy? Why are you my mom? Why is it called a bird?" Every single day was fascinating and wonderful.

The root of the word "wonderful" is "wonder." We were full of wonder and awe, living in the experience. We were in the moment. That's not true today. Now we have to schedule intimacy into our relationship. What kind of world are we living in that we actually have to schedule a "date night" with our spouses or our lovers? That's not the relationship of someone who's enjoying the journey of life. That's an activity-driven person who's going from one line of the to-do list to the next. Relationships have in many ways become like an old friend we bump into. What's missing is the joy of living, of breakthroughs, of the redesigning process. What's missing is the joy of the moment when something wonderful is happening, or that moment where we know we've made a mistake, but we also know we can learn a valuable lesson from it.

Are you living in joy, harmony, and love? If not, what could possibly be more important? As human beings, we have the opportunity to live in a state of joy, a state of learning, and a state of connection. We have the opportunity to live in a state that allows us to create, moment to moment, new opportunities for ourselves. We can transform breakdowns into breakthroughs. We can transform obstacles into opportunity. In the movie *Dead Poets Society*, Robin

Williams' character tells his high school students, "*Carpe diem*, boys. Make your lives extraordinary." So what would it take to turn the ordinary moments into something extra-ordinary?

We've all heard the expression, "Is the glass half-empty or half-full?" Let's take that further. Many people engage in life from the standpoint of being a victim. And a victim is engaged in life from the standpoint of having no responsibility. What does the word responsibility mean? Try this: Response-ability. The ability to respond. If I'm responsible, then I'm the author of my life. I am the source. I am the cause. I hold the power. I can use my power to affect, to change. I can use my power to make a difference. So, in response to that age-old question, I ask: Who poured the glass in the first place? What did you put in it? Why did you leave all the extra space? Maybe the space is there to remind you of all the room there is for you to create new possibilities.

As we discussed earlier in the book, life is not a game of perfection. Life doesn't always work out the way we want. Sometimes we're blindsided by a sour lemon when we were expecting to sink our teeth into something sweet. Maybe you were committed to losing twenty-five pounds in six months, but you only managed to lose fifteen. Maybe you were committed to expanding your profitability by 10%, and you only managed to expand by 1% that year. These are the realities of life. The reality of the journey is that it doesn't always work out the way we want. So imagine if we could transform the way we relate to those breakdowns, the way we relate to those challenges, and the way we relate to things not going the way we wanted them to go. How can we do that? It's simple.

We look at a challenge as a gift. We look at it as an opportunity—an opportunity to learn, an opportunity to grow, and an opportunity to reinvent ourselves, to redesign ourselves. What if there were no accidents and everything that is happening in your life is happening for a reason? What would that reason be?

As I mentioned earlier, I play golf. The game of golf can act as a perfect mirror for life. I assert that the way people play golf is exactly how they live their life. Sometimes you're playing very well, and then you hit a bad shot. Out of nowhere, a bad shot. Maybe you're in the trees or in a sand trap. Obviously, when you hit that bad shot, you have a choice. How do you respond? How do you react? Do you become a victim? Do you get mad at yourself, use all of your energy to beat yourself up for hitting a bad shot out of nowhere? Or do you look at this as an opportunity for you to accept and embrace what it is? You hit a bad shot. So what if you're in the trees? So what if you're in the bunker? What are you going to do about this? How can you turn this breakdown into an exciting and creative possibility? Anyone can hit a great golf shot from the middle of the grass fairway, without obstacles. But what about hitting a low hook, up and over the creek, over the sand, and not too far, so that it stays on the green and lands near the hole? Wow, the ESPN play of the day!

When you're able to change your attitude and perspective, to decide not to waste energy beating yourself up, and you're able to look at the situation as an opportunity, you can go into these very challenging situations—in the woods or the water or the sand—and find a way to make a shot happen. You can create something in that moment that you never thought you could. How exciting is that? What if there was an inner James Bond, Batman, or Mac-Gyver in all of us?

It winds up being a gift. It winds up being an incredible opportunity. At the end of the round, even if you end up with a really good score, you won't care, because the only thing that matters is the shot you hit out of the woods. All that matters is the shot you hit out of this horrible situation that you didn't think you could handle. You pulled it off because you had the ability to see it as an opportunity, the ability to tap into your creativity. You responded to the situation you were dealt. What were your other choices? The only real truth about being in the woods is that you're in the woods. What you do in the woods is completely up to you.

We live in a society that embraces success and the joys of our life accomplishments. But when things get rough, or when things don't go the way that we want them to, then we're no longer in the journey, we're no longer embracing it. Instead, we automatically think, "I'm the victim in this situation. Why is this happening to me? Who can I blame, who can I assign fault for this breakdown? Get me out of here, I quit." We often look back into the past, see through our historical limiting beliefs, and use our current failures and breakdowns to validate and feed those old conversations.

If we could transform ourselves to live in the journey of failure the same way we do in the journey of success, we would strengthen our connection to life. We would also shorten the time between the breakdowns and the breakthroughs. When I'm with other people and I'm asked the standard question, "How is your wife?," I have an opportunity in that moment to get off autopilot, to check in and connect with the question. Or I could answer automatically and simply say, "She's fine." I choose to look at my genuine feelings and answer it authentically, expressing how I truly feel. That's how you live in the moment. That's how you live in the journey. I love my wife Hillary more than I ever thought was possible in a romantic relationship. She continuously blows my mind on a daily basis. I admire and respect her. She's the most kind, generous, and beautiful woman I've ever known. I am blessed to be in this relationship. Imagine you are asked a similar question, and you take a moment to check in with your feelings. Speaking from authenticity gives life to the relationship. It doesn't minimize it. How many times have you heard someone say "the wife," in reference to their own? "The wife wants me to bring milk home." Those words sound like nails on a chalkboard to my ears. Who wants to be in a relationship like that? Clearly, he has lost the spark, the passion, the newness, the joy, the connection, or is simply on automatic. Can you imagine her experience?

In so many relationships, it's not the big issues, such as infidelity, that kill the love. It's the inappropriate use of sarcasm, the way you miss beautiful daily moments when your mind is elsewhere. It's holding onto small mistakes your spouse makes: leaving the dirty clothes on the floor, leaving the toothpaste cap off, not putting the toilet seat back down, or leaving mascara on the counter. Over time, we become numb, and in some cases, bitter. These situations can be resolved by basic communication, honesty, and making simple requests. "Talking over texting" is my motto, and it's the key to a healthy relationship.

Now, if a big breakdown happens, maybe a huge failure or disappointment, or even a painful loss, what would be possible if you gave yourself permission to experience the pain, suffering, or frustration? To release those emotions? If you need to cry or scream or let out your emotions because they're eating away at you, then go for it. That's a healthy way to live. You can't just choose to give in to only happy emotions. Have you ever heard a young child say things like, "I need my coffee before I watch TV. I'm not a morning person," or "Thank God it's Friday. Life is hard. I'm so stressed out," or "I refuse to play with Robert anymore. He sabotaged my relationship with Ashley; I'll never trust again." You would never hear these comments from a young child because they would never say them. Who needs coffee? ADULTS DO!

Why do children have so much natural energy? It's because they experience their emotions fully at all times. When they are finished, they let it go. They don't make up interpretations that cause them continuous pain or stress. How often do you cry? I believe a healthy human being has the capacity to be moved to tears each and every day. Whether they're tears of joy or tears of pain, you're giving into a cleansing experience, which is essential to living. I can literally just look into my sons' or daughters' eyes and cry out of simply connecting with my love, gratitude, and pride. My daughter Savannah and I play a game where we make eye contact and see who can cry first. Crazy? Maybe. Just like Beyoncé, I'm crazy in love. Even Larry will squeeze a teardrop out every now and then.

It's important to experience the journey, each and every part of it. Don't miss a moment. Learn how to take those breakdowns and turn them around by accessing your power, your responsibility, and your creativity. Look at every small failure as a gift instead of a curse.

Happiness is something that we generate. Joy is something that we create. People are joyful when they're following their vision, when they're proud of themselves. I don't mean "proud" in the sense that our egos need to be stroked constantly by other people. I'm talking about that deep sense of inner pride we get when we're living our visions, when we're being authentic and true to ourselves, when we're taking committed action that's consistent with the vision that we declared, when we're walking the talk. When you're around people like that, you see it in their eyes, in their energy, and in their way of being. They don't even have to talk for you to feel it. They just walk into the room, and you can feel their energy instantly—you can see it, and you know you want to connect with and be near that person. You're hoping that some of their magic will rub off on you.

Sometimes, tragedies will occur in our lives. For example, people die every day in this world. People are in crisis. Maybe we have friends and family who have lost their jobs. Maybe we have friends and family who are serving in Iraq or Afghanistan and aren't at home with us right now. We all have goals in life that we didn't achieve. We all have breakdowns in communication with our loved ones. While writing this part of the book, I received notice that an old friend had passed away. I found out the news from a text. Wow.

Living in a constant state of happiness can sometimes be interrupted by real events and human experiences that we all go through. These are not things that you can control. The nature of life and living is that inevitably, people die. It's a painful and emotionally difficult experience for anyone and everyone to go through. Often, when we lose someone special to us, our natural instinct is to go through the process of grieving. One of the first steps in the grieving process is to be angry. The more you try to control the anger, the worse it gets. Being in denial and suppressing your emotions never resolves pain or suffering—it actually makes the feelings worse and they can become toxic and permanent.

When we do not allow ourselves to naturally experience our feelings, we shut down and shut off our desire and willingness to share our emotional selves with people. We retreat back into our comfort zones. We build walls around ourselves by creating an imaginary suit of armor to shield and protect us from the perceived pain. We tell ourselves that it's safer behind the walls when the source of the pain is on the other side. Is that true? If you're feeling pain but don't allow yourself to experience it, will it ever go away and get better? If you're in a state of numbness, if you're experiencing essentially nothing, is it permanent or is it temporary?

In the work of transformation, I have discovered that "THE ONLY WAY OUT IS THROUGH!" When we are courageous enough to face and even confront our pain, we have the power to LET IT GO. What is the true value of experiencing your pain, no matter how hard or uncomfortable it may be? You can reclaim who you are and reopen your heart to the world around you. Going through this emotional cleansing will allow us to reconnect with the joy of love, life, and living. Joyfulness is one of the highest forms of being, and it is available to all of us regardless of our conditions or circumstances.

Even in a joyful experience, we can find tears, breakdowns, and moments of sadness. But you relate to these moments from a responsible place, and from that responsibility, you can turn it into a breakthrough and get yourself back on track, continue to create the life you want to live.

A horrible incident occurred in South Carolina during the summer of 2015. A white man walked into a church and took the lives of young people who were in a prayer meeting. The man murdered the people because they were African Americans. This was an evil act of racism, hate, and bigotry. Three days after the murders took place, the families of the victims were interviewed and showed great vulnerability, grace, and forgiveness for the man who committed the crimes.

Even in extraordinary situations and circumstances, we must find the strength to experience our feelings, cleanse our spirits, and reconnect with our power to affect change and create a life worth living. Denying pain perpetuates pain. Experiencing pain resolves pain!

You can take concrete steps as you're pursuing your visions, while simultaneously experiencing the journey. I want to introduce you to a tool that I refer to as a Personal Strategic Plan (PSP). This is not a to-do list. A PSP is based on specific, actionable steps and a well-thought-out method to carry out your ultimate goals, and of course, your vision.

Successful businesses have business plans, and within their business plans, they are constantly adapting and adjusting to the trends and to the environment. This will require a process of checking in regularly to see what's working and not working. As a result, you might need to set and reset your goals, strategies, and methods. I invite you to take the time to create a PSP for your life that is aligned with your vision. Your PSP will include all areas of your life: personal relationships, family relationships, business, finances, time management, health, recreation, travel, etc.

For example, maybe you want to go back to school and complete your degree or get an advanced degree. Maybe you want to communicate at a higher level in your marriage. Maybe you're ready to take a risk and begin a new romantic relationship. Maybe you want to meet new people and create new social opportunities. Maybe you want a new career. Maybe you want to achieve better health, lose weight, and build muscle strength. Maybe you want to save money, invest for your future, or maybe you want to write a book of poetry. The possibilities are endless.

Let's sit down and take the time to create your Personal Strategic Plan. Begin by writing your vision at the top of the page. Now write your personal mantra, beginning with "I am a _____." Next, make a list of the areas of your life in which you are committed to achieving extraordinary results. Declare your immediate short-term and long-term goals and commitments in each of the individual areas. Make sure you know the distinction between a goal and a commitment. A goal is something specific that you want to achieve. A commitment is something specific that you'll do no matter what. For example, maybe your goal is to lose fifty pounds because you want to be healthy and empowered, and want to feel great about life and living again. Your commitment, on the other hand, is to lose twenty-five pounds in the next twelve months. Maybe your goal is to be married with 2.5 children and a two-story house with a white picket fence within the next five years. Your commitment would be to start dating, to identify the key components you're looking for in a romantic relationship, and to be rigorous in choosing a partner who shares the common vision with you.

Your goal is something you really want, something you're passionate about having and achieving. Goals automatically empower and inspire you. If you were to succeed, it would transform your life and help you accomplish creating a life worth living. But with a goal, you're not quite willing to put your word at stake. Obviously you still want it to happen, but wanting it and being committed to it are not the same. When you make a commitment, you *are* putting your word at stake. You're saying you will do this no matter what, that you are committed to making it happen. You will honor your commitment and honor your word. You will not stop until you get the results. You will do it by a certain deadline you've set for yourself, never after.

Let's say your goal is to be closer and more connected to your wife. Your overall goal and strategy is to take your love relationship to a higher level of intimacy. You can make a commitment to be in communication with her daily, regardless of your circumstances. No matter where you are working in the world, you will make sure to create a connection with your wife for a minimum of five minutes, a minimum of ten minutes, a minimum of an hour, or whatever is functional based on your daily responsibilities and availability. It needs to be something you can do every day no matter where you are. Sometimes you're together and sometimes you're traveling out of town, but that commitment is present every day, no matter what. You have given your word to create this loving and intimate connection regardless of circumstances, including time or distance. Not only is it your word, but your word comes from your desire to experience the magic of love with your wife and to give her the connection she desires, as well. This committed action is aligned with your vision and the journey you're passionate about creating.

By following through on the commitments in our PSPs, we develop completely new habits in living our lives and moving in the direction of our visions. Our habit is no longer comfort. Our habit is no longer survival. Our habit is no longer settling for mediocrity. Our habit is no longer inventing a great story or excuse to justify ourselves when we fail to follow through with achieving our goals.

Instead, our new habit is excellence and bringing the future into the present. We feel really good about ourselves when we accomplish these daily commitments, and as a result, we create momentum—winning is infectious. So naturally, we are hungry to do it again tomorrow.

Here's an excellent example of momentum. My wife works out five or six days every week, sometimes even seven days a week. She does it because she feels good about herself when she does. She's empowered. With each new workout, she is riding the momentum from her previous workout session. She also works out on those days when she doesn't feel so good. She will even work out when she's physically ill. Why? How? Because she is vision-driven and has made a commitment to her health. It's as if it's going to happen no matter what, and when that consistent behavior occurs, the vision starts to become more and more real. She has established her new comfort zone, which is excellence in health. She doesn't need any type of outside push or motivation. Instead, she's driven by her own natural fuel to create a life worth living.

We can make short-term commitments, whether they are for business, our personal lives, relationships, health, or finances. Maybe you want to save money, and right now, you can afford to save $50 a week. What do you do? You give your word to save for a certain amount of time, no matter what. Just as you cut checks for your rent and/or mortgage, you also put $50 away each week into a savings account. This money can't be touched or else you haven't kept your commitment. That's $200 a month, or $2,400 a year. Ten years from now, what will that $2,400 be worth if it has been invested in a savings account or an IRA? It could become a substantial amount of money that you can use to build towards the trip of your dreams, your child's college tuition, or your retirement on the beach in Florida.

A lot can be accomplished if you make small commitments on a daily and weekly basis that will move you towards those greater goals and commitments. Remember, a goal is something you want, something you're passionate about, something that is aligned with your vision, but you're not quite willing to put your word at stake to pursue it. Are you still going to work towards it? Yes. Do you want it badly? Of course. Is it important to you? Absolutely. Are you taking action? Most definitely.

But that's still not the same as giving your word. Your word is at stake when you publicly put yourself on the line for it. If you're committed to something, then you're giving your word that you will make it happen by this time, or on this day. No stories, no excuses, no justifications. You can either have results in life, or you can keep making those excuses. Remember, we've wasted a lot of time in our lives. From getting up to getting ready, to just about, to getting out there, to someday, to hopefully, to when the grass gets greener, when men change, when women change, when we elect a new President, get a new boss, in the next year, etc. We waste a lot of time making excuses and telling stories instead of taking committed action.

When we are committed to something, the story no longer matters, the excuses don't matter, and your circumstances don't matter. When you commit to something, you're aligned with your vision in every way of being. Every action you take moves you towards achieving that commitment, and you won't stop until you have the results.

By the time you do get results, you're on fire and ready to go for the next level of achievement. Imagine you're about to get on the Space Mountain ride at Disney World, and you have a chance to change your mind and get off until the safety bar comes down. When the bar comes down, what does that mean? It means you are locked into the commitment and the choice you made to go on the ride, and whether you like it or not, you are on the ride until it's complete. How you feel, and whether you enjoy the ride, is entirely up to you, but not seeing the ride through is no longer a choice. You are 100% committed. Can you imagine being committed to your life and your PSP at that level? You will create extraordinary results, and I bet you'll discover free time you didn't know you actually had.

No matter how committed and vision-driven you are, everybody will experience setbacks from time to time in the journey of life and living. Sir Richard Branson, who you'll remember is creating a spaceplane to take passengers into space, dealt with a deadly crash during a test run. This was an enormous setback for his company. It was a very public breakdown. Twenty years ago, it wouldn't have been a big story. But twenty years ago, the news wasn't on twenty-four hours a day, seven days a week, and there was no such thing as social media. Many people may not know that Branson once tried to fly a hot air balloon around the world and also failed back then. When we think of Richard Branson, we might even think that he isn't capable of failing. We're so used to associating his name with extraordinary success.

But Richard Branson had a huge setback, and everybody was talking about the failed test run. Video footage of the crash was repeated over and over on every single news channel. This was a marketing nightmare for a business that is still in the vision and development phase. But even though he experienced this major setback, it wouldn't stop him from seeing his vision through. He came right out afterwards and acknowledged the sadness he felt for the pilot who lost his life. He also pledged his commitment to taking care of the pilot's family and doing whatever it took to help them heal from their tragic loss. Nonetheless, he reaffirmed to everyone that this was part of the process of realizing his vision. He has made this commitment and will not stop. Given the deep sense of caring and compassion he has for his employees, the pilot's tragic and unexpected death will certainly haunt him more than a setback for his company. Maybe Branson's attitude and worldview will assist the family of the deceased and all involved in the healing process. Everyone knew the risks involved in this endeavor. The pilot was doing what he loved, living his own vision at the time of his death. Behind the scenes, I assume there was a lot of commotion going on, and not just for the families that were affected. I'm certain there was heartbreak, devastation, anger, and frustration from all sides. As we established earlier, expressing emotions is a natural state of being human. When tragedy occurs, it's time to let the river flow.

In life, everybody needs to have their occasional "Dennis Rodman moments," as I like to call them. Dennis Rodman was a professional basketball player in the NBA who was probably more famous for his ranting and venting than for his actual play. He fully experienced his emotional state from moment to moment. While he didn't always behave professionally or manage his emotional releases in an effective way, there's nothing inherently wrong with venting. There's nothing wrong with emoting. There's nothing wrong with releasing pain. What are your alternatives? If you're mad, be mad. If you're sad, be sad. By acknowledging your feelings and allowing yourself to release those emotions, you can eventually let them go.

Anger and frustration are completely human reactions to failures and setbacks. It's normal to have feelings, to want to express them and let them out. What we need to do is find a healthy environment to do it in—and a healthy way to do it. For example, you could talk to a friend. You could talk to your husband or your wife. Maybe you would feel more comfortable with a coach or a therapist. Whatever method you choose, everybody needs to find an outlet to release the anger, frustration, and emotion. Let out the pain; let out the hurt.

It's important to find someone who's going to show empathy, compassion, sensitivity, and maybe even someone who'll agree with everything you say while you vent your frustration. You don't want to vent to someone who is challenging you at every turn and saying things like, "Well, that's not true," or worse, judging you, or not even listening to you. If you're sharing something really uncomfortable or painful about your husband, your father, or your boss, you need to find someone who will open up the space for you to express yourself in a way that is safe and devoid of judgment.

One of the most valuable steps you can take is to participate in one of the extraordinary transformational workshops that I run. For example, we have a training center in Puerto Rico called Impacto Vital. The trainings are an excellent tool for you to use to vent, release, and let go. But you can also use them to transform your future, just like I have. I strongly recommend participating in one of the workshops as soon as possible. There are several other centers across the U.S., in Latin America, and around the world. I work with some of the best: MITT in Los Angeles; Espacio Vital in Phoenix; and WE in Madrid, Spain. You can search the internet to find more information on the center nearest you.

We all need the ability to blow off steam without fear of disagreement. If you can communicate those negative emotions effectively to other people, so that they "get" your point of view, then you can begin to let it go. You can let go of your emotions, your frustrations, and your disappointments—everything that's stopping you from being present and enjoying the journey. You are essentially clearing the emotional debris in your mind.

When we say that someone "gets" us, it doesn't necessarily mean that the other person agrees with our opinions. To "get" someone's communication means to receive it, to listen, to show empathy, compassion, and understanding. When people feel heard, they can let something go. When people feel like somebody else understands them, they can let it go. Until that happens, people will hold onto those feelings and they may never be released. When you were a young child and got hurt playing outside, you specifically looked to your mother (or a similar figure in your life) for comfort, to give you a hug and a kiss, but more importantly, to "get" what you were going through. Everybody needs someone who can validate their experience.

Athletes have to go through this process constantly. The teams that win championships, the ones that are known as the greatest in their respective sports, still lose games. They still have bad days. Baseball is an excellent example. There are 162 games in a baseball season, and a championship team usually loses about seventy to eighty games before they finally win the World Series in October. Can you imagine losing seventy or eighty games a year when you're considered the best team in the world? With a 60% winning percentage, you can be considered the best team. That's how the game of baseball works. I believe life can be viewed in much the same way.

In life, we will sometimes make mistakes, and come up short. We will experience dejection and rejection. Does it really serve you to take the results personally? To resist the emotional upset? Holding onto the pain, trying to control it, will not support us in getting back into the game of life with confidence. The momentum will swing in the direction of insecurity, a lack of belief in our ability to achieve the desired goals. They will feel out of reach and seem like an impossible mountain to climb. You see this happen in sports all the time, like when a baseball player goes into a hitting slump. You can tell by his energy, the way he walks and carries himself. You can also see it in the way he swings the bat. He suddenly becomes very tentative, and he can't tell the difference between a ball and a strike when the pitch is coming to the plate. He can even affect the way a pitcher throws to the catcher.

There was once a pitcher for the St. Louis Cardinals who was unable to throw the ball accurately to the catcher. Instead, he was throwing the ball in the dirt and into the fence behind home plate. It was actually painful to watch as a fan. It wasn't possible to watch without feeling sorry for him, and he was clearly embarrassed and ashamed. He completely lost his confidence. After about a year of working on his throwing technique and his mental issues, it was clear his pitching days were over. The best part of the story is that this player, whose name is Rick Ankiel, reinvented himself and redesigned himself as a position player. He has since gone on to produce a productive career playing in a completely different position. The Cardinals even won a couple of World Series with him playing center field. You, too, can rebound from your breakdowns and transform yourself into a new version of you. If you were to let go of your previous strategy, game plan, and position in life, what would you choose to play? In which new direction could you take your life?

Sometimes it's hard to let go of the things that matter to you—the things you've decided are important—even if they're not. It doesn't matter whether this is a dream career, a relationship, an invention, a belief, a point of view, or your basic habits. Clearly there is a difference between holding onto your daily morning routine—such as the way you shower or dress yourself for work—and holding onto a relationship long after the love has died. Take a hard look at the things you hold onto in your life, the things that are holding you back or keeping you small. What would it take to transform them? Is it possible?

Sometimes letting go of something that matters to us feels like a death. The emotions are similar, but even though it feels that way, it's only an emotion. The attachment is made up by our ego, which wants to control the outcome of things in our life. But sometimes, no matter how much we want to control the experience and the results, it's just not working. We must learn to let it go. We must realize the feeling of death isn't the same as actual death. When you were in college, how many times did you go out to a party, drink too much, and end up getting sick? Remember the thoughts you had right before you threw up, kneeling in front of the toilet bowl? It probably sounded something like this: "Oh my God, I feel like I'm going to die." Yes, it's a feeling—you feel like you're going to die because you're about to vomit. But feeling like you're going to die and actually dying are not the same thing. That feeling is an interpretation, it's a thought, and it's not real. What we're really saying is, "Oh my god, I'm totally out of control right now, and I don't like it!"

Thomas Jefferson once said, "The art of life is avoiding pain." This was spoken by a man who entertained approximately a hundred people for the last twenty years of his life in a non-stop party at Monticello, his personal home. When Jefferson died, he was broke and in debt. But no one can say he didn't live a full life. He certainly did everything he could do to avoid pain. The best way to avoid pain is to release it. Thomas Jefferson died on the 50th anniversary of the Declaration of Independence and the birth of the United States. Isn't it perfect and fantastic that he would die in the middle of this extraordinary celebration?

Let's go back to that roller coaster from before. I asserted that life is like taking a ride on Space Mountain. In the beginning, as it begins to climb, most people feel afraid. We're experiencing a tremendous sense of fear and it makes us tense up. We start grabbing and holding onto the safety bar as tightly as possible. But once the ride gets to the top, all of a sudden it starts going down, and those very same people who were holding on for their lives now have their hands all the way up the air, enjoying every second. Many are screaming at the top of their lungs. When the roller coaster finally comes to a stop, those same people who were thinking to themselves, "I hate this. I'm going to die," are now saying, "That was awesome! I want to do it again!" Why? Because fear and excitement, fear and passion, fear and energy—they're two sides of the same coin. When you're afraid, your focus is inward on survival and self-preservation. When you're passionate and full of energy, your focus is outward towards creating your vision, creating a life worth living, and getting to the next branch of that tree.

The worst thing we can do when we're afraid is do nothing. We need to learn how to transform and release our fear into courage. Martin Luther King, Jr. once said, "Courage is action in the face of fear." When we feel fear, often we become paralyzed and frozen. When we take action in the face of that fear, we become courageous. When we become courageous, we become confident. When we become confident, we become powerful. When we become powerful, we become risk-takers. When we become risk-takers, we're moving on up to the Skinny Branches of the tree, and now we're inspiring other people to do the same.

Life is a journey. Immerse yourself. Celebrate the highs, and allow yourself to fully experience and release the lows. Every breath you take is a new moment. What other choice do you have?

Chapter Six

GOING OUT ON YOUR LIMB

WHEN YOU REACH THE TOP, you know you have arrived on the Skinny Branches. You're living the life you've always wanted, you're creating extraordinary results, you're experiencing the joy of being alive. You know how it feels to be free, to live a life of passion and courage. You are the sole uncontested author of your life and your life choices. You are no longer limited by your ego conversations or by interpretations from the past. You are living your inner mantra and making powerful and bold declarations. You are not going to allow anyone to clip your wings, including yourself. You are appreciating every moment, both big and small. You are present in your relationships, and you are connecting with the world around you. Have you arrived? Are you finally at the top? Now that you have reached the top of the tree, is there anything else? Is there another level? Is there a new step to creating a higher level of consciousness? Yes, absolutely.

When successful human beings achieve the highest level in their field of work or their life, they often lose their humility. Their ego conversations—however unwanted—return, like the robot in the movie *Terminator*. Just when you finally think he's gone forever, he shows up again. Sometimes, as a result of our successes, we lose our edge. We slow down, stop risking, and we become complacent. When you are on top of the tree and have finally reached the Skinny Branches, it's not time to stop. In fact, it's the perfect time to begin again. Can you stop to appreciate yourself for what you have achieved? Of course. It's essential to celebrate the manifestation of dreams coming true. When you acknowledge and appreciate your accomplishments, you actually create space for new energy, new openness. This is when life can really become exciting.

The highest level of living on the Skinny Branches of the tree is showing others how to climb. It's giving them the gift you once received. Remember that when Albert Einstein was asked what he thought the purpose of life was, he answered, "Life is a gift and if we agree to accept it, we must contribute in return. When we fail to contribute, we fail to adequately answer why we are here." Notice what he didn't say? He didn't say, "Life is a bitch, life is hard, life is about survival of the fittest, life is about greed, life is to win at all cost." It's time for all of us to contribute in return for the gift we were given.

Now that you are on top, you have nothing more to prove. You have only to give. To share your wisdom, distinctions, and authentic ways of being with as many people as possible. When you give of yourself to others, you not only make a difference in the world, you may even empower future leaders and creators. You actually create a culture shift. This shift could lead to a whole new society and civilization. How do you know your son or daughter isn't the next Steve Jobs, Amelia Earhart, or Nelson Mandela? You may have lifted yourself all the way up to the top of the tree, but do you want to be there alone? Do you want to be by yourself as you bask in the glow of living the life you've always wanted? It wouldn't make any sense. Imagine if what drove you was the knowledge that you could make a contribution to other people's lives in such a profound way that they reach that same level of the tree, or maybe even a higher level? Is there enough space around you for others to shine, too?

The Irish playwright George Bernard Shaw once said, "This is the true joy in life, the being used for a purpose recognized by yourself as a mighty one; the being a force of nature instead of a feverish, selfish, little clod of ailments and grievances complaining that the world will not devote itself to making you happy. I am of the opinion that my life belongs to the whole community and for as long as I live, it is my privilege to do for it, whatever I can. I want to be thoroughly used up when I die, for the harder I work, the more I live. I rejoice in life for its own sake. Life is no brief candle to me, it is a sort of splendid torch that I've got a hold of for the moment and I want to make it burn as brightly as possible before handing it on to future generations." Take a moment to digest his words, to immerse yourself in their possible meaning, as it pertains to purposeful living. Mr. Shaw lived until he was 96 years old, and he continued to write plays and books and participate in social activism until his death. He was the only author to win both a Nobel Prize for Literature and an Oscar for Best Adapted Screenplay, for the movie *Pygmalion*. He also refused to accept knighthood from the King of England. He was an inspirational leader with his words and his actions. He was celebrated and honored with countless awards, most of which he declined to accept. There was an element of humility in his work and his legacy. Everybody wakes up in the morning, but most people don't wake up thinking and focusing on other people and the difference they can make in their lives. If what drove us was the knowledge that we could make a contribution to other people's lives, our own lives would change, and the experience of living would change with it.

Most people give in short bursts, in fleeting moments. Most people give sometimes, but most people don't give as a way of life. People are giving during Christmas time, during birthdays and special holidays like Mother's Day, Valentine's Day, and Thanksgiving. Imagine if we were to create an environment, a new culture, in which people choose to give as a way of life. A place where people give without needing to, without the promise of getting anything in return. Without the expectation of receiving something in return. We would give just to give.

When I think of my daughter Savannah, I think of everything I love about her: her beautiful green eyes, bubbly personality, ear-to-ear smile, laugh, sensitivity, vulnerability, passion, wit, sense of humor, and intelligence. I see what's possible, not what's missing. I can honestly say that her outer beauty is her ugliest quality. And believe me, she is drop dead gorgeous. (Clearly, she got that from me, ha ha.)

Meanwhile, in my relationship with my wife, I focus on giving to her and empowering her in each moment we are together. I challenge myself to come up with new ways to express my love and gratitude. I consciously choose to declare it daily, to create a new level of love, intimacy, and joy. I'm surely not operating on autopilot.

When you're focused on giving to the people you care about the most, you are forced to transform your relationship with fear to the point where the fear no longer exists. You don't feel it. You spend your time thinking about contribution, about giving, and about making a difference, whether that means putting a smile on a stranger's face at Starbucks, creating a meaningful relation-ship with your wife, or reaching out to a friend in need. If you don't have the time to talk, you will make the time, because you know how much it means to the other person. Imagine what would be possible, not only in our everyday relationships and our life experiences, but in our communities, our country, and the world itself. Can you visualize living in the context of giving?

We may not yet be living a culture of giving, but Americans are amazing in a crisis. We are always willing to rise to the occasion. Look back through our history and you'll see how often we were willing to show our caring and our compassion, and to give generous aid to people in need, here and around the world. Where were you on September 11, 2001? It was a day that we will remember forever. We experienced the tragic loss of thousands of Americans who died in the World Trade Center, the Pentagon, and on the hijacked planes. When this horrific event happened, how did America respond? We stood together, put our differences aside, and reached out our hands to help our brothers and sisters get back up. When the tsunami happened in the Indian Ocean in 2004, approximately 230,000 people lost their lives. What did America do? We raised 1.8 billion dollars for aid and relief.

Can we give? Yes, we can. And look at the impact we make when we give. We can always be counted on in a crisis. But what if it didn't take a crisis for us to give? What if giving was as important as survival, as important as the air we breathe, as important as food, water, clothing, and shelter? Let's imagine that the society we live in is now based on a culture of giving. It starts with the way we behave in our own families—the way we talk to each other, the way we treat each other daily. If we teach our children the importance of giving, what difference will it make in the quality of their lives?

My definition of the word "give" is to generously inspire visions everywhere. If we give, we can create an environment where people see themselves as connected to the rest of the world, where we spread inclusion and trust instead of fear and separation. Einstein once said, "A human being is a part of the whole called by us universe, a part limited in time and space. He experiences himself, his thoughts and feeling as something separated from the rest, a kind of optical delusion of his consciousness. This delusion is a kind of prison for us, restricting us to our personal desires and to affection for a few persons nearest to us. Our task must be to free ourselves from this prison by widening our circle of compassion to embrace all living creatures and the whole of nature in its beauty." Take a moment to connect with what it means to "embrace all living creatures." Wow, this thought could stop people in their tracks and cause a profound shift in the way they see the world around them.

Giving can show up in big ways and in little ways. Giving can come in the form of showing love and affection for your children, empowering them to believe in themselves, to express their creativity, and to dream about the future they desire. Giving could also be participating in a local soup kitchen on a random Sunday, not only on holidays like Thanksgiving. Giving could be paying for the toll or the coffee of the person behind you in line. Giving could be starting a non-profit organization—like the One Campaign, which Bono started—to help make poverty history. Giving could simply be the act of walking a senior citizen across the street and helping her with her bags. Giving is a context, a way of being, an attitude of generosity, abundance, empowerment, and love.

A few years ago, I was eating dinner at a restaurant, celebrating the completion of a leadership workshop I had facilitated. I was feeling a great sense of elation, joy, and fulfillment over the difference I had just made with the students in the course. I was thinking about how magnificent and magical they are as people, based on their individual breakthroughs and the tools they now possessed, and how they were going to apply them to their lives. I was imagining their visions for their personal and professional lives coming to fruition. Given that I had just worked for about sixty hours over the previous five days, and in an incredibly intense process, you would think I'd be tired, but I wasn't. I was exhilarated. It was the kind of feeling you might have after an intense workout in the gym, only this was more significant because it involved transforming people's lives.

During the meal, our server was a man named Carlos, and I immediately became interested in connecting with him. I found out that he was a Mexican immigrant who migrated to the United States when he was sixteen years old. He entered the country illegally, in desperate search of an opportunity to work and make money. At this point, his story was not unlike many similar stories you may be familiar with from your own experiences. But there was something unique and compelling about this man. He was not only an excellent waiter—one of the best I've had—but there was something in his eyes, his tone of voice, his way of being, that made me curious and want to know more. Have you ever had an experience like this with a stranger you've met while out and about in life? Some unexplainable force made me want to connect with him, to get to know him, to understand him and hear the rest of his story. I asked him a lot of questions about his life, his work, and his family. I listened very intently as he spoke. The questions caught him by surprise, but he responded humbly and shared very openly. He opened up to me without defensiveness, apprehension, or distrust. It's beautiful to meet a man who is willing to be honest with a complete stranger. I don't see other people in conversations like this very often, but I love to strike one up on a regular basis. It's something I think I might've gotten from my father, Roger. He is an extremely social person, always willing to talk to anyone. Impromptu conversations with strangers may be unusual in the world we live in, but not in the world I live in, nor in the world I want to create on the Skinny Branches of the tree. I couldn't possibly miss the chance to pursue a deeper connection and understanding with Carlos. In our conversation, I discovered that he takes care of his family, including his wife, their two children, their grandchildren, and his extended family back home in Mexico. He also told me he worked seven days a week in two different jobs and hadn't had a vacation in his entire life. You heard me correctly—he had never had a vacation in his entire life. He and his wife never even had a honeymoon. Sounds like a very sad story, right? But you shouldn't, even for a moment, feel sorry for this man and his life choices. Why? There was not one ounce of resentment in his voice, not one ounce of manipulation, not one ounce of complaint. He was one of the most gracious, humble, and thankful people I have ever met. He shared his story with me from a place of great pride, great love, and great appreciation for what he has, and for what his purpose is in life. He wasn't asking me for anything. He didn't want anything more than he had. He only wanted to give generously to his family and to the world around him. He told me that everything in his life is a blessing. And we've all heard people say that before, but we could also tell that they were being inauthentic. They were just trying to convince themselves that they were embracing their life situations, but the words weren't sincere. Carlos meant what he said. He understood about *giving as a way of life.*

As a result of connecting and listening to Carlos, I was compelled and naturally committed to doing something for him. I was enamored with the gift he is to the people in his life, and you can now count me as one of those privileged people. I took out my checkbook, unbeknownst to him, and wrote him a personal check for $500. You should have seen the look on his face when I gave it to him. He saw the check and immediately began to cry, which also made me cry instantly. He reached over and gave me the biggest, most tender, and loving hug, as if we were friends for life. I wrote on the check, right there on the memo line: "Honeymoon with wife." Initially, he refused to accept the check, but I responded that he could not refuse a gift when a gift was given. I made it clear to him that he wasn't allowed to be giving, generous, and kind to everyone he meets in the world, and then be selfish when it comes to receiving. It's not fair. So in the end, he accepted my gift. Why did I do it? What were my motives? I simply wanted to acknowledge the beautiful gift Carlos had given me through his way of being. The sparkle in his eye and the genuineness of his heart were completely inspiring to me. I wanted to give back and did it without expectation. On top of the gift I gave him, I gave him the customary tip for my meal. I always tip based on my experience of the person serving and whether they are giving in their serving. The more they give the more I want to give back. Giving can create a cycle—what goes around comes around.

When I returned to my hotel room, I lay in bed feeling an incredible sense of gratitude. Gratitude for the life I was living and the choices I was making. I had the realization that making a difference doesn't stop or end when a workshop is complete. Anyone can do a job, or play the part of leader and giver, like it's a performance or an act. I choose to live up to the highest potential for myself as a human being and use the power and influence I have to empower the world around me. This includes not only my friends and family, but strangers, too. What were our friends before they became friends? Strangers. A stranger is a friend you haven't met yet. What if the next time you enter an elevator, instead of doing what everyone else is doing, instead of staring ahead at the door or the floor indicator, you turn directly to the others, make eye contact, and say, "Hi, how are you? Where are you from? What are you up to today?" Or maybe you can even take a bigger risk and say, "Wow, you're beautiful. I love your dress. You have a great smile." I know it sounds crazy, and maybe it kind of is. But somehow and some way, we have the opportunity to make a meaningful difference with people. This can manifest itself in many ways. In the moment, it may not seem substantial, but it could one day make a significant contribution to someone's life.

What can you see from the top of the tree? We've heard that the sky is the limit. But what if there really is no ceiling? Just a never-ending blank canvas for creating new visions and dreams, for painting your masterpiece. No matter who you are, where you come from, what circumstances you have encountered, nothing is impossible for you.

One of my favorite books is *Oh, the Places You'll Go!* by Dr. Seuss. In the book, he writes, "Congratulations! Today is your day. You're off to great places! You're off and away! It's opener there, out there, in the wide, open air." Feel the wind in your hair, the breeze on your face, and let your imagination run wild, without limitation of time and space. Maybe there's a little Dr. Seuss in you, too?

One of my favorite memories from my son Nicholas' childhood are the moments when he would open up his birthday or Christmas presents. His blue eyes would bulge out of his head as he stared at the boxes. He loved Legos, and he could play and build for hours at a time. He was immersed in the creative process. I think artistic creativity must skip a generation. Clearly, he must have gotten his from my mom. His canvases were blank spaces, and his paints were plastic Lego bricks of all shapes and sizes. When he was around seven years old, we started buying him whole Lego systems. He would not stop building until the masterpiece was complete. Sometimes it took all day, sometimes even more, but he would barely take a break in between, even for food or sleep. When he was done building the Millennium Falcon or the Death Star, both from *Star Wars*, he would put the finished product on his shelf. He would play with the structure for about thirty minutes, but then it went on the shelf to stay. I would say, "Nicholas, don't you want to play with it now that you've taken all this time to build it?" But he would say, "No, I don't want anything to happen to it." What was he saving it from? A terrible hurricane? A mysterious flood? He simply loved the process of building—creating this spaceship from scratch, and then admiring it from a distance. Little did he know that inside I was thinking, "I know what toys are, and they are to be played with, not admired." But to my son, the entire creative process *was* his version of playing. Remember, we all have a little boy or girl inside of us, underneath all the layers of knowledge and experience. What would it be like if we could tap back into the spirit of our youth? Life is too short to take yourself so seriously. Give your vision air to breathe and bring it to life.

Remember the hundreds of people who have already spent $200,000 to reserve their spots on Sir Richard Branson's space-plane? Think about those people. These aren't only people who have the money to invest or money to burn. They are clearly visionary risk–takers, too. The aircraft hasn't even been finished yet. By declaring this vision of space travel, Branson has made it possible for other dreamers to play on his tree. This is a man who makes things happen, who lives on the cutting edge. He's much more interested and invested in the possibilities of the future, in climbing to the next level of the tree, than in living off of past accomplishments.

Martin Luther King, Jr. needed more time and contemplation before climbing out onto his Skinny Branch. When he finally took the risk and stepped up, he stood up in front of not only a crowd, but the whole country. When you're a fiery and passionate speaker like Martin Luther King, it may look easier on the outside. But if you're an introvert, don't let that be an excuse not to express your dream to others. Remember, it's not always how you say the words or the volume with which you speak, it's where you are speaking from. You can be a soft-spoken person and still have a great vision, incredible wisdom, and powerful words that people want to listen to and be inspired to action.

Gandhi was a slight man. He wasn't a passionate speaker with a sweet-sounding voice, but when he spoke, people listened to him. His words came from a genuine place of humility, and he was a man of character, always walking his talk. *Having* character trumps *being* a character. One of the great qualities of a visionary is the ability to be serious and yet know when to laugh at yourself. Gandhi was known to have an incredible sense of humor. If you read his writings, he spoke from his heart and mind with great intelligence and depth. And he had a great gift of using humor to deliver his messages. This was a very serious time of crisis in India, a life or death situation. Yet, laughter can sometimes be the best therapy, and Gandhi knew it. This is a man who embodied everything he stood for. He didn't just talk about peace—he was committed to creating peace on every level, regardless of challenges or struggles. His actions spoke louder than his words. Maybe you've heard this expression: "What you're not saying is so loud, I can't hear what you're saying."

When you're on the Skinny Branches, your inner mantra is heard in all of your behaviors and actions. Are you able to laugh at yourself? Do you have a sense of humor? The ability to laugh and make light of your everyday challenges can be inspiring to you and the people around you. Laughing can reduce stress and tension, and it actually releases chemicals in your body that will possibly allow you to live longer. Part of giving is not only to have fun, like a consumer, but to *be* the fun for people in your life.

Think of how many comedians have allowed us the opportunity to laugh at our silliness and our ridiculousness as human beings. They make a profound difference, not only by creating laughter, but also by forcing us to think about how we live our lives, and maybe by empowering us to make different choices. The comedians who have had a great impact on my life include Richard Pryor, Eddie Murphy, Robin Williams, Jerry Seinfeld, Bill Maher, and one of my all-time favorites, George Carlin. He even gave me an opportunity to laugh while I was writing this book. He once said, "I went to a bookstore and asked the saleswoman, 'Where's the self-help section?' She said if she told me, it would defeat the purpose." Now that's funny! Humor is one of the most empowering ways to give to the world around you. How often do you make people laugh? I don't mean making them laugh *at* you, I mean making them laugh *with* you. *Let's laugh all the way to the top.*

Living on the Skinny Branches is not the same thing as crossing a finish line. It's more like reaching a new level. After achieving a personal record time, every runner has only one intention—to beat that time the next time they race. It's part of human nature to compete, not only with ourselves, but with others. To push ourselves to the edge of what's possible. Look at it from both a professional and a personal point of view, and set new goals and new commitments after each success.

People are often so busy that they can't stop. That's also true when we're empowered, excited, and creating extraordinary results. Sometimes we're so caught up in the experience that we don't stop, don't re-evaluate, don't think about changing direction or rethinking the vision. It's important to do this on a consistent basis. Once you're on fire and you have momentum, once you're on the Skinny Branches and you're creating a life worth living, make it a point to stop and figure out what's next. Have any new possibilities presented themselves?

Once the Skinny Branch gets too comfortable, it's not really a Skinny Branch anymore. For example, public speaking is now in my comfort zone. It wasn't in my comfort zone thirty years ago, but after three decades of practice with speaking in front of an infinite number of people—sometimes groups of thousands—I've achieved a new level of comfort. Thirty years ago, the thought of speaking in public was like having a needle stuck in my eye. It often felt like a fate worse than death. I wasn't alone either: In a survey once conducted about people's greatest fears, public speaking came in at number one. Death was number four on the list, to put it in context. But public speaking is now the base of my tree.

During the past thirty years, once I accomplished a certain level of success as a public speaker, I was able to learn higher levels of effectiveness in my communication. For example, I can actually deliver an entire seminar that lasts twelve hours per day, for five full days, all without using any notes. The information is not only in my mind, but firmly saved in my internal hard drive, to the point where I can invent and create fresh new ideas in the moment, all while simultaneously recalling the original context, distinctions, and content to be delivered. How is that possible? Thirty years of practice, yes. Rigor, yes. Commitment, yes. But it was also partly an internal surrendering process. It was my willingness to let go of my attachment to what I know, to step into the unknown.

Living on the Skinny Branches of the tree gives me the freedom to access my creativity. I have vivid memories of my mother painting when I was a child. I remember her holding the palette in her hand and dipping a paintbrush into the colors and swirling them onto the blank canvas. Often, I would look at the picture and have no idea what she was painting. When I asked her to tell me what it was, she would say, "Michael, what do you see? What do you think it is?" Honestly, I had no idea what it was most of the time. She was an abstract artist. She would try to explain to me that she was working with these specific colors and shapes. I remember thinking to myself, "Jeez, Mom. Can't you paint a vase, a person, a car, something I could actually see and understand?" Of course, I probably said it out loud, given my tendency to be a thorn in her side, but I desperately tried to recognize what it was and say something nice about it. Why was it so hard for me to understand? First of all, it was my mother, and if you remember from earlier in the book, I had my issues with her. But more importantly, our ego minds always need to match what we see with something we're familiar with in order to comprehend what's in front of us.

What if the purpose of art was much like the purpose of being on the Skinny Branches of the tree? What if the purpose is to willingly suspend reason, logic, and rational thought in order to allow yourself to find your own colors and shapes? After all those years of thinking my mother was a "nutty" artist, maybe she was actually a genius. Sometimes artists are misunderstood geniuses, and it can take generations for the world to recognize it. My mother was the ultimate master of limitless possibilities. She created something out of nothing on a blank canvas every day. A few days might pass, and when I saw her painting again, I'd ask, "Hey Mom, is this a new painting? What are you painting now?" She would say, "Nope, it's the same one." And I'd say, "Mom, it can't be, this one's completely different." I remember asking her, "How do you know when the painting is finished?" And she said, "It's finished when I feel it's finished." In the world of results, in school, sports, business, and life, as we were conditioned and trained to think, that response made no sense at all. But that's the beauty of art, isn't it? The same lessons can somehow be applied to the way we live our lives. We just have to find the place where it all connects together.

Let's say painting in your home is level one, painting in class is level two, showing your paintings in public is level three, selling your paintings is level four, and teaching others to paint is level five. When have you reached the top level? Maybe you never do. In the movie *The Mexican*, Brad Pitt's character asks Julia Roberts' character, "When you love someone and you both just can't seem to get it together, when is enough, enough?" Her reply is, "Never." Not only is that a completely romantic scene that leaves you diving for the Kleenex, but what if it's also true in all aspects of life? Each level requires a certain level of risk, confidence, and courage. Each level is a higher level on the tree. Think about your relationship, or the one you're committed to creating in your vision. When do you reach the highest level of love, intimacy, and connection? What if the answer is "never"?

Sitting next to me on the Skinny Branches of my tree is my wife, Hillary. Can you imagine opening a box of Cracker Jacks every day? Can you imagine the butterflies you had when you first fell in love? Can you imagine the most beautiful honeymoon experience? Can you imagine that each and every day together is better than the one before? I literally rub my eyes and pinch myself because I have found the pot of gold at the end of my rainbow. I have never had the privilege of meeting my heroes from the history books, but I am living with one. Hands down, Hillary is the most amazing person I've ever known. Every choice she makes is made with the purest of intentions. She just wants to make our world colorful, beautiful, and full of sunshine. She sprinkles love into everything she does. This is a woman who has the responsibility to raise three children and owns a business with over 200 employees. Either one of these commitments could be a full-time job for the average person, but not my wife. She is unlike anyone I know. She doesn't have a mean or evil bone in her body, only genuine goodness. She walks her talk, always keeps her word. I love her, like her, respect her, admire her, and of course, I am attracted to her, completely. How could I not be? She gets so much done for the whole family before I even get up in the morning. The one and only wish I have is for her to give to herself as much as she does for everyone else. She is my best friend, and I trust her implicitly. She is the first person I would go to for advice, both professionally and personally. Why? Her vision is clear, her values are impeccable, and she has the remarkable ability to find the light in any darkness. The bar is set impossibly high, but I am committed to elevating my game. One of my missions in life is to give her what she has given me. I've got a lot of work to do. But I'm living on the Skinny Branches, and the only thing that excites me more than what we have today is what we will create tomorrow.

In each and every conversation, we have the choice to give of ourselves. When we do, it's as if we get to experience what we've previously experienced once again, anew, through someone else's eyes. For example, let's say you go on a vacation to a place that you found to be heaven on earth. It could be anywhere—Hawaii, the Greek Islands, Rome, Barcelona, Puerto Rico. Even by mentioning these places, as I just did, I could have inspired someone to go for a visit. We have the power to cause change every time we open our mouths. It could be the depth of the content in communication, the excitement with which we say it, how much the other person cares for us, or the weight of our stamp of approval.

We move people. We move them up or down, but very rarely sideways. In which direction are you moving people? I believe that if you are on the Skinny Branches, you have the responsibility to move people up, so that they can join you. You have a responsibility to help them along the way, in their own journey. When you do, not only do you make a profound difference, but you get to access a part of yourself you didn't know existed. When you help them up, you move to a higher level of awareness, consciousness, and purpose. The contribution actually creates a new branch for you to aspire to.

Wake up in the morning and contribute. Wake up in the morning and live a life today that even you would be proud of. Bono, from the Irish rock group U2, is one of my heroes, and has been since I was sixteen years old. Bono grew up in Dublin, and when he was fourteen years old, his grandfather passed away. That day was a very traumatic experience for him because he felt very close to his grandfather. He felt like the two of them had shared a very deep relationship, and this was the first loss Bono had experienced in his life. But it got worse. While they were at his grandfather's funeral, his mother also unexpectedly passed away. After losing her dad, she was overwhelmed with pain and her heart actually stopped beating.

Now Bono had lost both his grandfather and his mother at the same time. Two of the most important people in his life were suddenly gone. He was emotionally devastated. And while all this was happening within his family, the city of Dublin was experiencing terrorism with the IRA fighting against the Protestants in Northern Ireland and the British government. There was terror in the streets, and bombs were going off. It wasn't safe. Many of his friends were in gangs and doing drugs. Bono has said that he could have gone the same route in an attempt to release his anger, but instead of doing that, he put all of his emotion into his music.

Thirty years later, U2 has won more Grammy Awards than any other band in history. Bono has been nominated for the Nobel Peace Prize twice. He has raised millions and millions of dollars for several different African countries in need. He has given to so many diverse causes: starting and supporting the One and Red Campaigns, which raise money for AIDS research and anti-retroviral drugs for HIV, creating jobs and businesses to end poverty, providing food to end famine, providing shelter for people to live in, providing tents for people to protect them from getting malaria, and many other services. He has no familial ties to Africa and is under no obligation to do any of this extraordinary charitable work; he simply chooses to do it. Many entertainers are egomaniacs who are selfish and self-destructive. They live in their own world. These celebrities spend most of their time focusing on glamour, fame, money, plastic surgery, partying, and of course, their favorite subject—themselves. There are many examples, take your pick. Bono and his U2 bandmates started playing music with each other when they were fifteen years old in high school, and they have been together ever since. No band has ever been as big or as successful as they are without a dramatic break-up or major breakdowns, including deaths. All of the great rock and roll bands have broken up: The Beatles, The Who, The Rolling Stones, Led Zeppelin, Aerosmith. U2 has never broken up. Bono is still married to his high school sweetheart. Most marriages last a maximum of seven years, and he's been married for over thirty years, has five children, and plays in a rock and roll band. Who does that? How is it possible? In general, rock and rollers are not known for being faithful to their wives. In fact, most have a reputation for the opposite. But Bono uses his power, credibility, and influence to make a difference in the world. He doesn't care how he looks or what people think. He is shamelessly committed to his vision.

In Germany during World War II, when the Jewish people were being loaded onto trains to be taken to concentration camps, many of the spectators stood by watching and did nothing as the trains pulled out. Bono says that we're essentially doing the same thing while millions of Africans are infected with HIV, dying of AIDS, or dying of poverty and famine. Every day, there are more than 5,000 Africans who die of starvation.

Another part of what makes U2 a great band are the lyrics in their songs and the messages behind their words. In one of their songs, Bono wrote, "Where you live should not decide whether you live or whether you die." The music and lyrics are inspirational not only to me, but also to millions of U2 fans throughout the world. Most of us don't stay in touch or maintain any meaningful relationship with our childhood friends, except once in a while when we see them at reunions. U2 began their relationship as teenagers and have not only a business relationship, but also a deep personal relationship that has stood the test of time and life. After almost forty years together, they have been both on top of the world and at the very bottom, but they did it standing side-by-side every step of the way. They use their lives for a mighty purpose well beyond money, fame, and awards. They see it as their responsibility, their humble privilege, to use their status to step out on the Skinny Branches. Not only that, they want the rest of the world to join them—including everyone in Africa. Not bad for a group of rowdy punks from Ireland. What difference could you make if you used your passionate rebellious side to support a cause that positively impacts the world?

I recently saw the movie *The Theory of Everything*. What a remarkable story of the life and work of Stephen Hawking. After seeing the movie, what did I do? Did I leave the theater and say, "Hey, that was such an amazing movie. I'm going to keep it to myself, and it'll be my secret?" No, of course not. I thought, "Who else would love this movie?" The answer to that question was, "Everybody!" So, where did I start? I wanted everybody I know to see this movie so I could share this experience with them. I reached out to my brother Larry. He was so excited by what I had to say that he took his wife and all of their kids to see the movie immediately that night.

Even though I had already seen the movie, I couldn't wait for my brother to see it so we could share his experience. Why? To make a difference in his life, because giving to the people we love is natural, and it should be easy, like breathing air. When he shared his point of view with me, I learned something new, just from listening to him. His perspective opened up new possibilities for even greater interpretations than I had for myself.

We can apply this same concept on a much larger scale. My wife is the owner of a successful business. What if she kept her knowledge to herself? She would be missing out on the opportunity to empower other people, to give to other people, to contribute to other people's lives and careers. Instead of keeping her experiences to herself, she could be inspiring other women who are mothers and wives. She could be helping them see that they have the power to be business owners and entrepreneurs, to use their own unique ideas, gifts, and ingenuity to start new businesses. And guess what? That's exactly what she does.

Hillary is the current president of the Fort Worth Chapter of the Entrepreneurs' Organization (EO). That's right, she's not just a member, she is the current president of the chapter. This organization has monthly meetings, during which a group of business owners get together to share their experiences with each other. They confide with each other regarding what's working and what isn't working in their respective businesses. They coach each other. They support each other. She's actually working in partnership with other business owners. She's learning from them, and they're learning from her. She's sharing what she has created on the Skinny Branches of the tree with other people who are also on their own Skinny Branches. And during this time, she's been one of only a handful of women involved with EO. Only a small percentage of entrepreneurs in the world are women, but she is one of them, leading the way up to the Skinny Branches.

I've had many mentors during my development as a coach and trainer. One day, one of the ones I respected most said to me, "Michael, you're the best leadership trainer in our company. However, you need to decide what's more important to you—to be the best at what you do, or to take the next step and become a master?" I asked him what the difference was, and he told me that masters have the ability to create the same level of expertise and wisdom in someone else. They pass down their knowledge and their experiences so that another person can become as competent as they are—maybe even surpass them one day.

When I heard that, the light bulb above my head lit up. I could see that this was my opportunity to create the next level on my Skinny Branch, which was not only to be a star but also to become a star maker. It was an entirely different experience for me. Everybody is different. I don't always have the answers, but I don't need to have all the answers. The process of figuring out how to bring out the star in each individual is a welcome and exciting challenge for me. I have the opportunity to discover new skills and form new levels of coaching, new tools, new methodology, new processes, and of course, new connections with extraordinary leaders.

If you've already been living on the Skinny Branches for some time, and you're looking for that next level, focus on being a star maker, a master. Mentor those who are still struggling to find their Skinny Branches. One day, they might even surpass you by using what they've learned through your guidance as a springboard. The most fulfilling experience in life is the ability to give others the opportunity to access their highest version of themselves. To empower them to discover what's possible on the top of their tree. You aren't perfect, but when you're on the Skinny Branches, your vision is. You get to leave a legacy that you will be infinitely proud of as you live your life with no regrets—heart wide open, at full throttle, courageous and free.

It is an honor and a privilege to be alive, to have the opportunity to declare your vision and create a life worth living. I am infinitely blessed and grateful for the first fifty years of my life, and I can't wait to boldly step up to the next branch of my tree.

Skinny Branch living is available to everyone. What are you waiting for? Open your eyes and open your heart. Go for it! Leave it all out on the field—you can't take it with you when you're gone. Passionately give the gift of you.

TO LIVE IS TO GIVE.

ABOUT THE AUTHOR

MICHAEL STRASNER IS ONE of the most respected leading experts in personal and organizational transformation. Through his mastery of coaching and understanding the psychology of leadership and human behavior, he has been able to facilitate and design extraordinary workshops dedicated to the art of life and living on the Skinny Branches. During the last 30 years, he has worked with over a 100 thousand students and people from all over the United States, South America, and Europe.

Strasner has facilitated breakthroughs in leadership, business strategy, management, and peak performance workshops for Time Warner Inc., Merrill Lynch, Barclays Investments, The International Provident Group, Concordia Advisors, Taubman Company, Lord Associates, Altman Development Inc., Worldnet Telecommunications Inc., Coast Asset Management, Prolab Inc., Kaye/Bassman International, and many others. He has also delivered multiple keynote speeches for several companies, including one for Tacori Jewelry at the Beverly Wilshire Hotel, entitled, "Creating A Life Worth Living."

As an entrepreneur, Strasner has started several highly successful and profitable businesses. Through his passion for entrepreneurship, he has specialized in working with startup companies, and most importantly, the leaders who lead them. Two of his clients have won the highly prestigious Ernst & Young Entrepreneur of the Year awards.

Strasner's personal vision is to create a world of peace, love, unity, and abundance. This is reflected in the work he does in the domain of personal transformational training. He has also authored several workshops: Mastering the Art of Relationship, The Entrepreneurial Mind, Mastering Leadership for Teenagers (NSLC), The Masters Course (Rock and Roll edit), and the highly regarded L.P. Ph.D. Program. Through his commitment to creating leadership in others, he has mentored and developed dozens of world-class trainers and coaches, who are currently facilitating workshops globally.

In addition, Strasner has written articles on organizational transformation and leadership in business for the Caribbean Business Journal. He has also been a featured guest in newspaper articles, podcasts, and radio shows, sharing his expertise on such diverse topics as effective communication, connection and intimacy in relationships, building self-esteem, the power of authenticity, personality adapting through style flexing, powerful and impactful public speaking, and jump-starting your passion for life.

To find out more about upcoming workshops, seminars, or speaking engagements, you can visit his website at www.michaelstrasner. com.